THE WIT & WISDOM
OF THE
ROYAL FAMILY
A BOOK OF ROYAL QUOTES

Edited by Marianne Sinclair and Sarah Litvinoff

Plexus, London

The wit and wisdom of the royal family
    1. Great Britain. Royal families, 1895-
    I. Sinclair, Marianne II. Litvinoff, Sarah
941.085′092′2

    ISBN 0–85965–176–2
    ISBN 0–85965–116–9 Pbk

Phototypeset by Input Typesetting Ltd, London
Manufactured in Great Britain by Hollen Street
Press, Slough
Cover design by Design Box
Book design by Madeline Serre

CONTENTS

'The pleased incredulity with which the public reacts to the elementary demonstration on the part of Royalty that they are, after all, like other people is matched only by the public's firm refusal to accept them as such.'
The Duke of Windsor

1

GEORGE VI
&
QUEEN ELIZABETH

GEORGE VI

George VI was born on 14 December 1895 and christened Albert Frederick Arthur George. He was the second son of the Duke of York, who became George V. 'Bertie,' as he was called by his family, had the misfortune to be born on the 34th anniversary of the death of Prince Albert, whose mourning widow, Queen Victoria – Bertie's great grandmother – was still very much alive.

'Rather distressed that this happy event should have taken place on a darkly sad anniversary.' *Queen Victoria*

Bertie's childhood was not a very happy one. He lived in the shadow of his elder brother Prince Edward – 'David' – who was destined to be King, and who was brighter and better looking than Bertie. His mother was rather cold and aloof in her dealings with the children.

'I have always to remember that their father is also their King.' *Queen Mary*

Bertie's father was also rather severe.

'My father was frightened of his mother, I was frightened of my father, and I am damned well going to see to it that my children are frightened of me.' *George V*

It is not surprising that this is the letter that Bertie's father wrote to him on his fifth birthday:
'Now that you are five years old, I hope you will always try and be obedient and do at once what you are told, as you will find it will come much easier to you the sooner you begin. I always tried to do this at your age and found it made me much happier.' *George V*

Bertie was born left-handed, and his tutors set about forcing him to use his right hand. The strain gave him a stammer which afflicted him throughout his life, and also affected his progress. When Bertie was six his tutor wrote:
'I really thought we had mastered division by three but division by two seems to be quite beyond [Prince Albert] now.' *Mr Hansell*

Although he was considered slow by most, those who took time with Bertie found the truth quite different.
'I found that far from being backward he was an intelligent child with more force of character than anyone suspected in those days.' *Lady Airlie, family friend*

Later his legs were put into splints to cure his knock-knees.
'I am sitting in an armchair with my legs in the new splints and on a chair. I have got an invalid table, which is splendid for reading but rather awkward for writing at present. I expect I shall get used to it.' *George VI, when Prince Albert*

The splints hurt so much that his manservant would sometimes loosen them for him. But George V got to hear of it and went into a fury. He showed the manservant his own knock-knees.
'If that boy grows up to look like this it will be your fault.' *George V*

At the age of fourteen Bertie entered the Royal Naval College at Dartmouth, but after a short while he caught whooping cough and spent three months convalescing. Soon after returning, his father became King, and Bertie's performance went from bad to worse.
'My dear boy this will not do. If you go on like this you will be bottom of your term.' *George V*

His childhood left Bertie cowed and nervous, but a very good and obedient son.
'Very different to dear David.'
George V

Bertie was bottom of his class – 68th out of 68 – and the next year improved his position by only one place. When he passed out of Dartmouth he came 61st out of 67.

'Quite unspoiled and a nice honest, clean-minded and excellent mannered boy.' *Final report from Dartmouth*

Bertie was in the navy when war broke out, but after being operated on for appendicitis he was declared unfit for active service. However he was well enough to go back to sea by May 1916, when his ship was caught up in the Battle of Jutland.

'I never felt any fear of shells or anything else. It seems curious but all sense of danger and everything else goes except the one longing to deal death in every possible way to the enemy.' *George VI, when Prince Albert*

Bertie continued to suffer with his health and eventually had to be operated on for a duodenal ulcer, after which he stopped active service. But war had made Bertie more confident and less dependent on his family.

Bertie was picked on by his fellow cadets, who liked to say that they had kicked the son of the King, or pricked him with a pin to see if his blood was blue. He was shy, stuttered badly and had big, sticking-out ears.
'Bat Lugs.' *Bertie's nickname at college*

—— QUEEN ELIZABETH ——

The Queen Mother was born Elizabeth Angela Marguerite Bowes-Lyon in London on Saturday 4 August 1900. She was registered late by her father, Lord Glamis (he had to pay a penalty of 7/6d), who stated incorrectly on her birth certificate that she had been born at St Paul's Walden Bury, the family home. Elizabeth was her parents' ninth child – she had blue eyes, a round pink face and tufts of dark curly hair.

'An exceptionally happy, easy baby; crawling early, running at thirteen months and speaking very young.' *Clara Knight ('Allah') her nanny*

On 2 May 1902 Elizabeth's mother gave birth to a baby boy called David.
'They were almost like twins.' *Lady Elphinstone (the Queen Mother's sister)*

'The two Benjamins.' *Family nickname for Elizabeth and David*

'Princess Elizabeth.' *Family nickname for Elizabeth*

'Buffy.' [from Elizabuff] *David Bowes-Lyon's nickname for Elizabeth*

'I was very impressed by the charm and dignity of a little daughter, two or three years old, who came into the room . . . as if a little princess had stepped out of an eighteenth-century picture.' *The Duchess of Atholl, family friend*

In February 1904, Elizabeth's grandfather died, and her father became the fourteenth Earl of Strathmore. Elizabeth was now a Lady. She was a demure, clever little girl who had great poise.

One day, aged four, she greeted one of her parents' employees:
'How do you do, Mr Ralston? I haven't seen you look so well for years and years.' *Lady Elizabeth*

Elizabeth's childhood was idyllic. She wrote about it in the form of a story when she was in her twenties.
'At the bottom of the garden is *The Wood* – the haunt of fairies, with its anemones and ponds and moss-grown statues, and the big oak under which she reads and where the two ring-

The two Benjamins had a secret hideaway in the loft of the flea house. David described what they hoarded there:
'a regular store of forbidden delicacies, acquired by devious devices . . . apples, oranges, sugar, sweets, slabs of chocolate, matches and packets of Woodbines.' *David Bowes-Lyon*

doves contentedly coo in their wicker-work "Ideal Home". There are carpets of primroses to sit on and her small brother David is always with her . . . Now it is time to go haymaking, which means getting very hot in a delicious smell. Very often she gets up wonderfully early – about six o'clock – to feed her chickens and make sure they are safe after the dangers of the night. The hens stubbornly insist on laying their eggs in a place called the *Flea House*, and this is where she and her brother go and hide from Nurse. Nothing is quite so good as the *Flea House*, but the place called the *Harness Room* is very attractive too. Besides hens there are bantams, whose eggs-for-tea are so good.' *Lady Elizabeth*

In 1905 a new governess came to teach the younger children and stayed for six years. This was her first impression of Elizabeth:
'An enchanting child with tiny hands and feet and rose-petal colouring, murmuring with perfect politeness, "I do hope you will be happy here." '
'*Madé', Mademoiselle Lang, the governess*

Pointing out a footman at a party:
'That's James, I'm going to marry him when I grow older.' *Lady Elizabeth*

The little Lady Elizabeth was sometimes naughty. Once she cut up a pair of sheets with her new pair of scissors.
Questioner: 'What will mother say?'
Lady Elizabeth (unconcerned): 'She will say, "Oh, Elizabeth." '

Asked to write her favourite pastime in an autograph album she wrote:
'Making friends.' *Lady Elizabeth*

Once, when her pocket money did not stretch far enough, she sent a telegram to her father.

'SOS LSD RSVP Elizabeth.' (LSD was the abbreviation for pounds, shillings and pence.) *Lady Elizabeth*

She was found another governess, this time a German woman called Kathie Kuebler, who liked her new charge very much:
'Charming to look at, a small delicate figure with a sensitive, somewhat pale little face, dark hair and very beautiful violet blue eyes . . . a child far more mature and understanding than her age warranted.' *Kathie Kuebler*

After a family entertainment in which Elizabeth had taken part:
'On being asked . . . the name of the character she had adopted, said with great *empressement*, "I call myself the Princess Elizabeth." ' *The Minister of Glamis*

'She was an ideal sister, original and amusing – and always full of fun or sympathy, whichever you happened to need.' *Lady Rose Bowes-Lyon*

In September 1912 David was sent away to school, leaving his sister very distressed.
'David went to school for the first time on Friday. I miss him horribly.' *Lady Elizabeth*

The First World War broke out when Elizabeth was fourteen. Four of her brothers joined up and one sister started to train as a nurse. Elizabeth was caught up in the preparations:
'The bustle of hurried visits to chemists for outfits of every sort of medicine, and to gunsmiths to buy all the things people thought they wanted for a war and found that they didn't.' *Lady Elizabeth*

'During those first few months we were so busy knitting, knitting, knitting and making shirts for the local battalion, the 5th Black Watch. My chief occupation was crumpling up tissue paper until it was so soft it no longer crackled, to put into the linings of sleeping bags.' *Lady Elizabeth*

The family spent their summers at Glamis Castle. Now Elizabeth moved there for the duration of the war. Much of the castle was turned into a hospital for wounded soldiers and Elizabeth used to spend a lot of time with them, comforting, playing cards or writing letters for them.

'She had the loveliest eyes, expressive and eloquent eyes, and a very taking way of knitting her forehead when speaking . . . that sweet, quiet voice, that hesitating yet open way of talking. For all her fifteen years she was very womanly, kind-hearted and sympathetic.' *One of the wounded soldiers*

THE ENGAGEMENT AND MARRIAGE

It is said that Elizabeth and Bertie first met at a children's party when she was five years old and gave him the cherry from her cake. But they came to know each other in the Spring of 1919, through his sister Mary, with whom Elizabeth was friends. It was at a dance in May 1920 that their relationship changed – at least so far as Bertie was concerned:

'He told me long afterwards that he had fallen in love that evening, although he did not realise it until later.' *Lady Airlie (family friend)*

Meanwhile, many more men were falling in love with Elizabeth.

'Her radiant vitality and a blending of gaiety, kindness and sincerity made her irresistible to men.' *Lady Airlie*

11

Shortly after this Bertie was made the Duke of York.
'Dearest Bertie . . . I feel that this splendid old title will be safe in your hands and that you will never do anything to tarnish it. I hope you will always look upon me as your best friend and always tell me everything . . . Yr. very devoted Papa.' *George V*

Elizabeth seemed to hold no particular preference for Bertie, though it was becoming obvious to all who knew him that Bertie was in love.
'I have discovered he is very much attracted to Lady Elizabeth Bowes-Lyon. He's always talking about her.' *Queen Mary*

In the Spring of 1921 Bertie told his father he meant to propose to Elizabeth.
'You will be a lucky fellow if she accepts you.' *George V*

Bertie proposed, and Elizabeth turned him down. Elizabeth's mother felt sorry for him:
'I do hope he will find a nice wife who will make him happy. I like him so much and he is a man who will be made or marred by his wife.' *Lady Strathmore*

But Bertie continued to see Elizabeth – and to be invited to stay with the Strathmores. A few months after he proposed he was writing from Glamis:
'Elizabeth is very kind to me. The more I see her the more I like her.' *George VI, when Duke of York*

Over the next year Elizabeth was proposed to by three or four suitors, but accepted none. Bertie refused to be deterred.
'Although the romance seemed at an end, he continued to plead his case.' *Lady Airlie*

'That winter was the first time I have ever known Elizabeth really worried. I think she was torn between her longing to make Bertie happy and her reluctance to take on the responsibilities which this marriage must bring.' Lady Strathmore

In January 1923 Bertie was determined to try again. He told his parents that if he succeeded he would send them a telegram. On 13 January it arrived:'All right Bertie.'

'We are delighted and he looks beaming.' *Queen Mary*

'I am very very happy and I can only hope that Elizabeth feels the same as I do. I know I am very lucky to have won her over at last.' *George VI, when Duke of York*

'My dream has at last been realised. It seems so marvellous to me to know that my darling Elizabeth will one day be my wife.' *George VI, when Duke of York*

The court circular announced the engagement on 16 January 1923:
'I feel very happy but quite dazed. We hoped we were going to have a few days' peace first, but the cat is now completely out of the bag and there is no possibility of stuffing him back!' *Lady Elizabeth*

It was suggested that the ceremony be broadcast on radio, but this was vetoed:
'The service might be received by persons in Public Houses with their hats on.' *The Abbey Chapter*

'Dearest Bertie – You are indeed a lucky man to have such a charming and delightful wife as Elizabeth, and

They were married on 26 April 1923 in Westminster Abbey. The day dawned wet.
'The sun actually came out as the bride entered the Abbey.' *George V*

I trust you will both have many years of happiness together and that you will be as happy as Mama and I after you have been married for 30 years, I can't wish you more . . .' *George V*

The newly-weds spent their honeymoon at Glamis. Elizabeth immediately contracted whooping cough.
'So unromantic on your honeymoon.' *George VI, when Duke of York*

'There is not a man in England today that doesn't envy him. The clubs are in gloom.' *Chips Channon, friend of Elizabeth*

George V was a stickler for punctuality, but under the spell of Elizabeth he even forgave her chronic lateness. Once when she apologised for arriving at dinner after everyone else he said:
'You are not late my dear. I think we must have sat down two minutes too early.' *George V*

'If she weren't late she would be perfect, and how horrible that would be.' *George V*

'The better I know and the more I see of your dear little wife, the more charming I think she is and everyone falls in love with her.' *George V*

THE YOUNG FAMILY

In 1924 they moved into 145 Piccadilly, but when the Duchess was due to give birth in 1926 she went to stay with her mother at 17 Bruton Street. As was the custom of the time, a government official had to be in attendance to verify that the child was truly that of the Duke and Duchess.

'If there have to be gentlemen waiting outside my bedroom door I hope it's someone we know!' *The Queen Mother, when Duchess of York*

The baby was born on 21 April 1926, by Caesarian section.

'We were awakened at 4.00 am and Reggie Seymour informed us that darling Elizabeth had got a daughter at 2.40. Such a relief and joy.' *Queen Mary*

When the parents decided on the names Elizabeth Alexandra Mary for the baby, they had to clear it with the King.

'I am sure there will be no muddle over two Elizabeths in the family and there had been no one of that name in your family for a long time. Elizabeth of York sounds so nice, too.' *George VI, when Duke of York*

'I am so proud of Elizabeth at this moment after all that she has gone through during the last few days, and so thankful that everything happened as it should and so successfully.' *George VI, when Duke of York*

In October 1926 the Duchess insisted that the Duke go to see a speech therapist called Lionel Logue so that he could learn to control his stammer.

'He entered my consulting room at three o'clock in the afternoon, a slim, quiet man, with tired eyes and all the outward symptoms of the man upon whom habitual speech defects had begun to set the sign. When he left at five o'clock, you could see there was hope once more in his heart.' *Lionel Logue*

'I have noticed a great improvement in my talking and also in making speeches which I did this week. I am sure I'm going to get quite all right in time, but 24 years of talking in the wrong way cannot be cured in a month. I wish I could have found him before, as now that I know the right way to breathe my fear of talking will vanish.' *George VI, when Duke of York*

When the Duchess became pregnant with her second child, she resolved to have the baby at Glamis. Everyone was convinced that the baby would be a boy, but on 21 August 1930 another little girl was born. The King vetoed their first choice of name: Ann Margaret, so they had to think again:
'Bertie and I have decided now to call our little daughter Margaret Rose, instead of Ann, as Papa does not like Ann – I hope that you like it. I think it is very pretty together.' *The Queen Mother, when Duchess of York*

In 1931 the King offered the Yorks the Royal Lodge at Windsor, which became their true family home. It was close to Fort Belvedere, the home of Bertie's brother the Prince of Wales, and they all used to meet up often.

Regarding her young family:
'I always like the term "family circle". It sounds so close, and safe and happy.' *The Queen Mother*

15

In 1932 the Duchess engaged Marion Craw-ford 'Crawfie' as governess for her daughters. Crawfie described her first impression of the Duchess:
'She had the nicest, easiest, most friendly of manners and a merry laugh. There was nothing alarmingly fashionable about her. She sat on the window ledge. The blue of her dress exactly matched the blue of her eyes. My whole impression was of someone small and quite perfect.' *Marion Crawford*

Elizabeth's recipe for her girls' education:
'To spend as long as possible in the open air, to enjoy to the full the pleas-ures of the country, to be able to dance and draw and appreciate music, to acquire good manners and perfect deportment, and to cultivate all the distinctly feminine graces.' *The Queen Mother, when the Duchess of York*

George V was more and more impressed by the York family, and increasingly disturbed by the company his eldest son and heir was keeping.
'I pray to God that my eldest son will never marry and that nothing will come between Bertie and Lilibet [Princess Elizabeth] and the throne.' *George V*

——— THE ABDICATION ———

George V died in January 1936, and 'David', formerly the Prince of Wales, was now Edward VIII. The Duchess had suf-fered a severe bout of pneumonia and was not entirely better.

'I am really very well now. I am only suffering, I think, from the effects of a family break-up, which always hap-pens when the head of a family goes. Outwardly one's life goes on the same, yet everything is different, especially mentally and spiritually. I don't know if it is the result of being ill but I mind things that I don't like more than before. But it will be very good for me to pull myself together and try to collect a little will power.' *The Queen Mother, when Duchess of York*

One of the main problems was that the new King was desperately in love with a once-divorced, still married American called Wallis Simpson. There were fears about what might happen if he wished to marry her. She and the Duchess did not get on. Once David and Mrs Simpson visited the Yorks to show off David's new car.
'I left with a distinct impression that while the Duke of York was sold on the American station wagon, the Duchess was not sold on David's other Amer-ican interest.' *Mrs Simpson*

'I didn't hate her. I just felt sorry for her by the end.' *The Queen Mother (quoted many years later)*

As the year wore on it became clear that the King was determined to marry Mrs Simpson after her divorce came through. In his memoirs David mentions a letter Bertie wrote to him.
'Bertie had most at stake. He wrote that he longed for me to be happy, adding that he of all people should be able to understand my feelings; he was sure that whatever I decided would be in the best interests of the country and the Empire.' *The Duke of Windsor*

The last thing the Duke and Duchess of York wanted was to be thrust on the throne, but as that possibility became inevitable, Elizabeth again went down with influenza caused by nervous strain. The King abdicated on 10 December 1936. Elizabeth was still recovering in bed when Queen Mary came to talk to her about the crisis.

'The Duchess had sent for me, and I stood outside waiting. Queen Mary came out and tears were streaming down her face. The Duchess was lying propped up among pillows. I thought she too had been crying. She held out her hand to me. "I'm afraid there are going to be great changes in our lives, Crawfie," she said. "We must take what is coming to us and make the best of it." ' *Marion Crawford*

THE KING AND QUEEN

'I never wanted this to happen. I'm quite unprepared for it. David has been trained for it all his life, whereas I've never seen a State Paper. I'm a naval officer. It's the only thing I know.' *George VI*

Elizabeth's first letter as Queen was to the Archbishop of Canterbury.
'I can hardly now believe that we have been called to this tremendous task and (I am writing to you quite intimately) the curious thing is that we are not afraid. I feel that God has enabled us to face the situation calmly.' *The Queen Mother, when Queen*

Bertie bestowed the Order of the Garter on his new Queen on his first birthday after becoming King. Afterwards Elizabeth wrote to Queen Mary:
'He had discovered that Papa gave it to you on his, Papa's birthday, 3 June,

'This can't be happening to me!' *George VI*

and the coincidence was so charming that he has now followed suit and given it to me on his own birthday.' *The Queen Mother, when Queen*

Many small things went wrong during the Coronation ceremony on 12 May 1937. Bertie wrote about them afterwards with exasperation and humour. The last one was nearly a disaster:
'As I turned after leaving the Coronation Chair I was brought up all standing, owing to one of the Bishops treading on my robe. I had to tell him to get off it pretty sharply as I nearly fell down.' *George VI*

The pace was hectic for the new King and Queen, who had led a moderately quiet life before. In 1939 they visited the USA and Canada. They travelled by boat, which came to a virtual standstill for a few days when they were surrounded by ice, approximately in the same place that the Titanic *sank.*
'I shouldn't have chosen an ice-field surrounded by dense fog in which to have a holiday, but it does seem to be the only place for me to rest nowadays.' *George VI*

Elizabeth did not find the atmosphere very relaxing when fogbound.
'Incredibly eerie, and really very alarming.' *The Queen Mother, when Queen*

During this tour Elizabeth was asked whether she was Scottish or English.
'Since we reached Quebec I've been a Canadian.' *The Queen Mother, when Queen*

The tour was a phenomenal success.
'That tour made us. I mean it made us, the King and I. It came at just the right time.' *The Queen Mother, when Queen*

The King was becoming used to public speaking, and his speech therapist had helped him work a miracle with his stammer.
'A change from the old days when I felt speaking was hell.' *George VI*

========

When someone mentioned that Wallis Simpson had done the Duke of Windsor a lot of good, and that he looked much better:
'Yes, who has the lines under *his* eyes now?' *The Queen Mother, when Queen*

========

On 3 September 1939 war broke out.
'I feel deeply for you, I have gone through all this in 1914 when I was wife of the Sovereign.' *Queen Mary*

George VI's first wartime Christmas broadcast included this quote, which was to become famous:
'I said to the man who stood at the Gate of the Year, "Give me a light that I may tread safely into the unknown." And he replied, "Go out into the darkness and put your hand into the Hand of God. That shall be to you better than light, and safer than a known way." ' *George VI*

Elizabeth practised using a revolver, should the enemy get as far as the Palace.
'I shall not go down like the others!' *The Queen Mother, when Queen*

London was regularly bombed, and the East End was the worst hit. The Queen regularly toured the bombed areas, giving sympathy and comfort. On one occasion she came across a woman distressed because her dog was trapped by some rubble, and she was trying to coax him out. Elizabeth took over successfully:
'Perhaps I can try. I am rather good with dogs.' *The Queen Mother, when Queen*

The Queen had new clothes made by Hart-nell, in the heartening colours of dusty blue, pink and lilac.
'Dusty is an apt colour. It doesn't show all the dust on bomb sites.' The Queen Mother, when Queen

On 13 September 1940 Buckingham Palace was bombed.
'I am glad we've been bombed. It makes me feel I can look the East End in the face.' The Queen Mother, when Queen

*The King, too, toured bombed areas.
Voice in the crowd:* 'Thank God for a
good King!'
George VI: 'Thank God for a good
people!'

*In the autumn of 1942 Eleanor Roosevelt,
the wife of the President of the USA, came
to stay in Buckingham Palace. She discovered the royal couple living on the same
austere rations as everyone else.*
'We were served on gold and silver
plates, but our bread was the same
kind of war bread every other family
had to eat.' *Eleanor Roosevelt*

'At Buckingham Palace we're very
careful to observe the rationing regu-
lations.' *The Queen Mother, when Queen*

'We do a lot of gardening at home.
The King is good at the digging and
the weeding. It is I who concentrate on
the secateurs.' *The Queen Mother, when
Queen*

*One night that same year a deserter broke
into the Palace and made his way into the
Queen's bedroom, where he hid until she was
alone then flung himself at her feet, held her
ankles and poured out his story to her.*
'For a moment my heart stood absolutely still. Poor man, I realised quite
quickly he meant no harm. I was so
sorry for him.' *The Queen Mother, when
Queen*

*On 7 May 1945 the Germans capitulated,
and when the news was made known the next
day huge crowds gathered at Buckingham
Palace, shouting for the King and Queen.*
'The Queen and I have been overcome
by everybody's kindness. We have
only tried to do our duty during these
five and a half years.' *George VI*

*In 1946 the Royal family visited South
Africa – the first and last tour that would
include the two Princesses as well as the
King and Queen: Princess Elizabeth had
been reluctant to come anyway because she
was in love with Prince Philip of Greece.
Boer veteran (during the trip):* 'Pleased to
have met you, Ma'am, but we still feel

sometimes that we cannot forgive the English.'

Queen Elizabeth: 'I understand perfectly. We feel very much the same in Scotland, too.'

After their return Princess Elizabeth became engaged to Philip, and they married in November 1947.

'They grow up and leave us, and we must make the best of it.' *The Queen Mother, when Queen*

The King had been anxious that the couple should not rush into marriage, and after the wedding he wrote to his daughter about this.

'I was so anxious for you to come to South Africa as you knew. Our family, us four, the "Royal Family" must remain together with additions of course at suitable moments! I have watched you grow up all these years

with pride under the skilful direction of Mummy, who as you know is the most marvellous person in the world in my eyes.' *George VI*

In 1948 the King and Queen celebrated their Silver Wedding.

'We were both dumbfounded over our reception . . . So many nice letters from all and sundry, thanking us for what we have tried to do all these years. It does spur us on to further efforts.' *George VI*

On 12 November 1948, two days before the birth of Princess Elizabeth's first child at Buckingham Palace, George VI had to have an operation because of an obstruction in the arteries in his right leg.

'The Queen was quite distraught with anxiety until the operation was over.' *Marion Crawford*

The Queen Mother loved her grandchildren, and was able to become increasingly involved with them.

'Half the fun of being a grandmother is being able to spoil your grandchildren.' *The Queen Mother*

The King continued to suffer poor health, with a further operation on his leg the next year, and real fears that he might have to have it amputated. Professor Learmouth, the doctor who attended him, was astounded when, during his final examination of the King, George VI whipped a sword out from under his pillow and knighted him with it.
'You used a knife on me. Now I'm going to use one on you!' *George VI*

On 23 September 1951, the King had an operation for lung cancer. On 31 January 1952 the King and Queen went to the airport to wave Elizabeth and Philip off on a tour of Australia, which was to encompass Kenya. Six days later, some time in the night of 5 February, George VI died in his sleep.

'One cannot yet believe that it has all happened, one feels rather dazed.' *The Queen Mother*

The widowed Elizabeth, now officially known as Queen Elizabeth the Queen Mother, was grief-stricken, but determined to carry on as usual.
'One must feel gratitude for what has been rather than distress for what is lost.' *The Queen Mother*

Congratulated on how well she controlled herself:
'Not when I am alone.' *The Queen Mother*

'Whereas everybody recognised how much the King had owed to his wonderful Consort, few people realised how much she had relied on *him* — on his capacity for wise and detached judgement, for sound advice, and how lost she now felt without him.' *Lady Cynthia Colville, family friend*

'Throughout our married life we have tried, the King and I, to fulfil with all our hearts and all our strength the great task of service that was laid on us. My only wish now is that I may be allowed to continue the work we sought to do together.' *The Queen Mother*

In June 1952 the Queen Mother first saw the Castle of Mey and fell in love with it and bought it soon after.
'A lovely little castle which was in danger of becoming derelict.' *The Queen Mother*

To Cecil Beaton about the castle:
'I've taken this villa to get away from everything; but I don't expect I shall ever be able to get there.' *The Queen Mother*

The Queen Mother also had to move out of Buckingham Palace to make way for the new Queen, and she took up residence in Clarence House on 18 May 1953. In October 1954 she embarked on her first solo tour, to the USA and Canada. She was such a success that the idea of the Queen Mother as Governor General of Canada was suggested.
'Oh, dear, we couldn't spare mother!' *The Queen*

When, after a surgical operation in 1966, a bulletin was issued saying the Queen Mother was 'comfortable'.
'There is all the difference in the world between the patient's meaning of the word and the surgeon's.' *The Queen Mother*

In 1972 the Queen Mother met the Duchess of Windsor for the first time for decades at the Duke of Windsor's funeral. There was no sign then of a feud between them.
'I know how you feel – I've been through it too.' *The Queen Mother*

THE REAL GEORGE VI

'Bertie has more guts than the rest of his brothers put together.' *George V*

'It is one of my main jobs in life to help others when I can be useful to them.' *George VI*

'His advice was so good and I could always count on [it] in times of difficulty.' *Winston Churchill, Prime Minister*

Teasing the artist John Piper:
'Why is it, Mr Piper, that it always seems to be raining when you do a sketch of Windsor? You've been very unlucky in the weather.' *George VI*

'Frankly, I don't like to see a play from the Royal Box. I'd far sooner sit where I can see the front only. I don't want to be peering into the wings to see who's coming on next.' *George VI*

THE REAL QUEEN MOTHER

'Ever since I can remember, my grandmother has been a most wonderful example of fun, laughter and warmth, and above all, exquisite taste in so many things. For me she has always been one of those extraordinary, rare people whose touch can turn everything to gold . . . She belongs to the priceless brand of human beings whose greatest gift is to enhance life for others through her own effervescent enthusiasm for life.' *Prince Charles*

'I'm not as nice as you think I am.' *The Queen Mother*

'It is so distressing to me that I always photograph so badly.' *The Queen Mother*

'The only regret one has as one grows older is that things do not matter so strongly.' *The Queen Mother*

Arriving a few minutes late from Buckingham Palace:
'Do please excuse me for being late but I've just been up the road having coffee with my daughter.' *The Queen Mother*

On meeting people now she is getting older:
'I must admit that sometimes I feel something flow out of me. It makes me feel very tired for a moment. Then I seem to get something back from the people – sympathy, good will, I don't know exactly, and I feel strength again. In fact recharged. It is an exchange.' *The Queen Mother*

Aboard the liner Queen Elizabeth, *an American passenger was sure he knew her face:*
Passenger: 'You advertise something – what is it?'
The Queen Mother: 'Oh it would be too unprofessional to tell you.'

'Traditions exist to be kept.' *The Queen Mother*

When she got a fishbone stuck in her throat and had to go to hospital:
'The salmon's revenge.' *The Queen Mother*

To a waiter at a banquet who dropped a sardine in her lap:
I promise not to say anything about this if you will bring me another.' *The Queen Mother*

Her way of saying no:
'Perhaps another time.' *The Queen Mother*

When the Queen asked for a glass of wine at a luncheon:
'Is that wise? You know you have to reign all afternoon.' *The Queen Mother*

'She has been the most marvellous mother – always standing back and never interfering.' *The Queen*

25

About helicopters, which she loves:
'The chopper has changed my life as conclusively as that of Anne Boleyn.' *The Queen Mother*

About the newly-built Hilton Hotel in Park Lane:
'I think you will find the Hilton is very much nicer if you look at it upside down.' *The Queen Mother*

On her refusal to grant any radio or television interviews:
'I'm sorry, I really can't. I am sorry to disappoint everyone, but I can't bring myself to do this.' *The Queen Mother*

On hearing the National Anthem on television:
'Turn down the sound. When you're not present it's like hearing the Lord's Prayer while playing Canasta.' *The Queen Mother*

On horse racing:
'It's one of the real sports that's left to us: a bit of danger and excitement, and the horses, which are the best thing in the world.' *The Queen Mother*

When asked during an official visit to an East End pub if she would like anything to drink:
'I think I would like to taste your beer.' *The Queen Mother*

Of the champagne she keeps in her thermos flask:
'It's one of my little treats.' *The Queen Mother*

Why she never wore a uniform during World War II:
'Some clothes do not like me.' *The Queen Mother*

Tactful way of rejecting new dress designs for herself:
'They are absolutely charming – but I think these are even more delightful.' *The Queen Mother*

Man complimenting the Queen Mother on her hat:
'It looks lovely from the back Ma'am.' *The Queen Mother:* 'I suppose I'll now have to walk backwards.'

'I like to have fun.' *The Queen Mother*

THE QUEEN MOTHER'S ROLE

'The work you do is the rent you pay for the room you occupy on earth.' *The Queen Mother*

'She has that quality of making everyone feel that they and they alone are being spoken to.' *Lord Harlech*

'I love meeting people. I have met people of every possible kind and it is so easy to get on with them after the first moment, isn't it? Nearly everyone is so pleasant. When one is eighteen, one has very definite dislikes, but as one grows older, one becomes more tolerant, and finds that nearly everyone is, in some degree, nice.' *The Queen Mother*

'I am terribly lazy and I always have to drive myself to do things.' *The Queen Mother*

'It's much more important not to miss anyone than to be five minutes late.' *The Queen Mother*

Talking of her wardrobe:
'My props.' *The Queen Mother*

On appearing in public:
'You must *never* look at your feet, my mother taught me that.' *The Queen Mother*

'One learns with practice how to do things better, such as seeing people who are at different levels in a crowd.' *The Queen Mother*

2

THE QUEEN
&
PRINCE PHILIP

THE QUEEN

The Queen was born Princess Elizabeth of York on 21 April 1926 at 17
Bruton Street, London W1. The first
child of the Duke and Duchess of
York, she was third in line to the
throne. At the time of her birth no one
seriously thought she would be Queen
one day, as her uncle, the Prince of
Wales, was heir to the throne and it
was believed that he would marry sen-
sibly and have children of his own to
follow after. The baby Princess was
delivered by Caesarian section, as she
was a breech baby.

'You don't know what a tremendous
joy it is to Elizabeth and me to have
our little girl. We always wanted a
child to make our happiness complete,
and now that it has at last happened,
it seems so wonderful and strange.'
George VI when Duke of York

'A little darling with a lovely com-
plexion.' *Queen Mary*

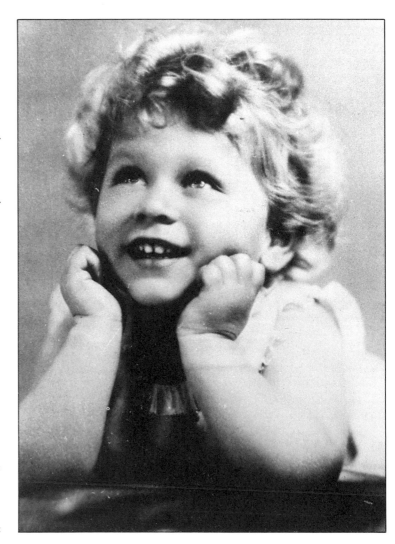

Elizabeth Alexandra Mary was christened on 29 May 1926.
'Of course poor baby cried.' *Queen Mary*

On 6 January 1927 the Yorks were sent on a six-month official tour of the Commonwealth and had to leave their baby daughter behind.
'I felt very much leaving on Thursday, and the baby was so sweet, playing with the buttons on Bertie's uniform it quite broke me up.' *The Queen Mother when Duchess of York*

The King and Queen, who helped to look after Princess Elizabeth while her parents were away, kept them informed about her progress:
'Your sweet little daughter has four teeth now, which is quite good at eleven months old.' *George V*

The pretty baby Princess soon became very popular with the crowds.
'It almost frightens me that the people should love her so much. I suppose that it is a good thing, and I hope she will be worthy of it.' *The Queen Mother when Duchess of York*

During Christmas 1929, when Princess Elizabeth was two and a half, she was listening to the carol 'While Shepherds Watched' with her grandfather George V, whom she sometimes called Grandpapa England, She was intrigued by the line 'to you and all mankind'.
'I know that old man kind. That's you, Grandpapa. You are old and you are very very kind.' *Princess Elizabeth*

'Lilibet.' *The nickname that Princess Elizabeth gave herself*

Of her early childhood:
'It was a time when the sun always seemed to be shining.' *Princess Elizabeth*

Princess Margaret Rose was born on 21 August 1930. Elizabeth liked her baby sister's name.
'I shall call her Bud. She's not a real Rose yet. She's only a bud.' *Princess Elizabeth*

Elizabeth was once walking down a corridor in Buckingham Palace with Queen Mary when they bumped into the Lord Chamberlain:
The Lord Chamberlain: 'Good morning, little lady.'
Princess Elizabeth: 'I'm not a little lady, I'm Princess Elizabeth.'
Later that day Queen Mary brought Elizabeth to his door.
Queen Mary: 'This is *Princess* Elizabeth, who hopes one day to be a lady.'

In 1933 'The Little Princesses', as they were known, were assigned a nursery governess, Marion Crawford (later to be nicknamed 'Crawfie' by the girls), a young woman with fashionably short hair. She later described her first conversation with six-year-old Princess Elizabeth, who was sitting up in bed holding toy reins, pretending to drive some horses.
Princess Elizabeth: 'How do you do? Why have you no hair?'
Marion Crawford: 'Do you usually drive in bed?'
Princess Elizabeth: 'I mostly go once or twice round the park before I go to sleep, you know. It exercises my horses.'

By 1936 George V died and his eldest son became Edward VIII. His constant companion was an American divorcee, Mrs Simpson, who was tolerated but not welcomed by the Yorks. She wrote about a tea party with them.
'The two little Princesses joined us. Princess Elizabeth, now Queen, was then ten, and Princess Margaret Rose was nearly six. They were both so blonde, so beautifully mannered, so brightly scrubbed, that they might have stepped straight from the pages of a picture book.' *Mrs Simpson*

'For goodness sake teach Margaret and Lilibet to write a decent hand, that's all I ask you. Not one of my children can write properly.' *George V to Marion Crawford*

The little Princesses loved to go swimming. George VI was amazed at their self possession amongst the other young swimmers.
'I don't know how they do it. We were always so terribly shy and self conscious. These two don't seem to care.'

Elizabeth gave advice to Margaret who was practising her swimming strokes on a bench by the side of the pool:

'Keep steady Margaret. You look like an aeroplane about to conk out.'

On being offered a book by a preacher:
'It's not about God, is it? I know all about Him already.' *Princess Elizabeth*

Elizabeth was always markedly well behaved.
'I remember how greatly struck I was by the way Princess Elizabeth's good manners survived even the fever of this most unfriendly game [of cards]. She would apologise for putting a card down in the way of one of mine. Once, to my astonishment, she even offered to take back her card.' *Lady Cynthia Asquith (family friend)*

By the end of the year Edward VIII had abdicated in order to marry Mrs Simpson, and Elizabeth's father became King George VI in his place. Crowds gathered outside their house on the afternoon of 10 December, and Elizabeth was told by a footman what had happened. She passed the news on to Margaret:
Princess Margaret: 'Does that mean you will have to be the next Queen?'
Princess Elizabeth: 'Yes, some day.'
Princess Margaret: 'Poor you.'

Margaret asked Elizabeth why the abdication was happening.
'I think Uncle David wants to marry Mrs Baldwin, and Mr Baldwin [the Prime Minister] doesn't like it.' *Princess Elizabeth*

'If I am ever Queen, I shall not allow horses to work on Sundays. They need a day of rest too.' *Princess Elizabeth*

History, geography, bible-reading and poetry were added to the Princesses' lessons.
'History is so thrilling.' *Princess Elizabeth*

'When I grow up I will marry a farmer. I shall have lots of cows, horses and children.' *Princess Elizabeth*

The Coronation took place on 12 May 1937 Elizabeth wrote an essay for her parents, entitled 'To Mummy and Papa. In Memory of Their Coronation, from Lilibet by Herself'.
'At five o'clock in the morning I was woken up by the band of the Royal Marines striking up just outside my window. I leapt out of bed and so did Bobo [her nanny]. We put on dressing gowns and shoes and Bobo made me put on an eiderdown as it was so cold and we crouched in the window looking on to a cold, misty morning. There were already some people in the stands and all the time people were coming to them in a stream with occasional pauses in between. Every now and then we were hopping in and out of bed looking at the bands and the soldiers. At six o'clock Bobo got up and instead of getting up at my usual time I jumped out of bed at half past seven.' *Princess Elizabeth*

The Little Princesses attended the Coronation in identical dresses and robes.
'They looked too sweet in their lace dresses and robes, especially when they put on their coronets.' *Queen Mary*

Elizabeth kept an eye on Margaret's behaviour during the ceremony.
I only had to nudge her once or twice, when she played with the Order of Service too loudly.' *Princess Elizabeth*

The Princesses learnt that they would have to leave their beloved house at 145 Piccadilly to go to live in Buckingham Palace.
Princess Elizabeth: 'What!'
Princess Margaret: 'Do you mean forever?'

She was worrying about Margaret:
'I hope she won't disgrace us all by falling asleep. *Princess Elizabeth*

'Now Margaret, be sure to copy me and you will be all right.' *Princess Elizabeth*

Elizabeth peering through the Palace railings at a boy riding past on a bicycle:
'One day I shall have a bicycle.' *Princess Elizabeth*

Her first reaction to life in Buckingham Palace when her father became King:
'People here need bicycles.' *Princess Elizabeth*

Instructions to Margaret before an official garden party:
If you see someone with a funny hat, Margaret, you must *not* point at it and laugh. And you must *not* be in too much of a hurry to get through the crowds to the tea table. That's not polite either.' *Princess Elizabeth*

With Margaret, saying goodbye to their parents who were off on a tour of Canada and the United States:
'Your handkerchief is to wave, not to cry into.' *Princess Elizabeth*

In July 1939 the little Princesses went with their parents to Dartmouth Royal Naval College, where Elizabeth – then thirteen – met Prince Philip of Greece, aged eighteen, for the first time. She fell in love with him there and then.
'She never took her eyes off him the whole time. At the tennis courts I thought he showed off a good deal, but the little girls were much impressed. Lilibet said, "How good he is, Crawfie! How high he can jump." He was quite polite to her but did not pay her any special attention.' *Marion Crawford*

In September 1939 Britain declared war on Germany. The Princesses were packed off to Windsor, while their parents stayed at Buckingham Palace.
'More history for people to learn in a hundred years.' *Princess Elizabeth's reaction to the outbreak of war*

The next year Elizabeth made her first radio broadcast, on a children's programme.

'I can truthfully say to you all that we children at home are full of cheerfulness and courage. We are trying to do all we can to help our gallant sailors, soldiers, and airmen, and we are trying, too, to bear our own share of the danger and sadness of war. We know, every one of us, that in the end all will be well.' *Princess Elizabeth*

'I don't think people should talk about battles and things in front of Margaret. We don't want to upset her.' *Princess Elizabeth*

About a murder case:
'What makes people do such terrible things? . . . One ought to know. There should be some way to help them.' *Princess Elizabeth*

In the spring of 1942, when she was sixteen, Elizabeth was confirmed.

'I saw a grave little face under a small white net veil and a slender figure in a plain white woollen frock. The carriage of her head was unequalled, and there was about her that indescribable something which Queen Victoria had.' *Lady Airlie (family friend)*

Throughout the war Elizabeth and Philip corresponded, and it was becoming clear to Elizabeth's family that this 'crush' was not going away. By the time she was eighteen Philip was beginning to return her affection, and some members of the family thought that they should be allowed to become engaged.
'We both think she is too young for that now as she has never met any young men of her own age. P. had better not think any more about it for the present.' *George VI*

Talking to her mother about her first lady-in-waiting:
The Queen Mother when Queen: 'She really can't come here like that! She must wear a hat!'
Princess Elizabeth: 'Don't be old-fashioned, Mummy. These days, many girls simply don't have a hat.'

On VE day George VI let his daughters mingle with the celebrating crowd around Buckingham Palace.
'Poor darlings, they have never had any fun yet.' *George VI*

After the war was over the King and Queen were still reluctant for Elizabeth and Philip to become engaged. They invited lots of other young men (nicknamed 'the Bodyguard') to meet Elizabeth, in the hope that one of them might interest her. Queen Mary was the only member of the family who thought that Elizabeth might be mature enough to know her own mind at twenty:
'She won't give her heart lightly, but when she does it will be for always. It does sometimes happen that one falls in love early, and it lasts forever. Elizabeth seems to me that kind of girl. She would always know her own mind. There's something very steadfast and determined in her – like her father.' *Queen Mary*

On the blossoming romance:
Queen Alexandra of Yugoslavia: 'I only hope Philip isn't flirting with her. He's so attractive and he flirts without realising it.'
Princess Marina: 'I think his flirting days are over. He would be the one to be hurt now if it was all just flirtation or if . . . if it's not to be. One thing I'm sure about, those two would never do anything to hurt one another.'

PRINCE PHILIP

Prince Philip of Greece was born on the dining room table of a villa called Mon Repos on the island of Corfu on 10 June 1921. His mother was Princess Alice, his father Prince Andrew of Greece. He was their fifth child and only son. Although he was born a prince of Greece, he was not Greek – he had Danish blood on his father's side and his mother was a great grand-daughter of Queen Victoria.

'They did not live like royals. We had a few untrained peasant girls to help, and two unwashed footmen who were rough fellows.' *Housekeeper at Mon Repos*

'His favourite toy was his nanny's pin cushion. For hours he sat quietly in his cot, pulling the pins and needles out and pushing them in again.' *Housekeeper at Mon Repos*

In 1922 the family were exiled from Greece, and Philip spent his childhood first in London then France, where his family, who were poor by royal standards, lived off the generosity of family and friends. His first memories are of his home in Paris.
'We weren't well off.' *Prince Philip*

On his childhood
'Not necessarily particularly unhappy.' *Prince Philip*

He was a good-looking, bouncy, blond child, who was very mischievous.
'He was a great show-off, he would always stand on his head when visitors came.' *One of Philip's sisters*

'A lively little lad.' *Housekeeper at Mon Repos*

'We four girls were very afraid his mother was spoiling him; she wasn't, but we felt that as he was the youngest, and a boy, he might be spoilt, and we were all very anxious to prevent it and were all particularly strict and dis-agreeable to him.' *One of Philip's sisters*

'Sometimes naughty, never nasty.' *Alexandra, his cousin*

'A nice little boy with very blue eyes.' *Queen Mary*

'He was like a friendly collie who never had a basket of his own.' *Alexandra, his cousin*

At the age of six Philip started at his first school, St Cloud in Paris.
'He was a rugged, boisterous boy, but always remarkably polite. He was full of energy and got along well with other children. He wanted to learn to do everything and asked at one time to be shown how to wait at table.' *Headmaster at St Cloud*

After this Philip spent three years at Cheam, the English preparatory school, where he shone athletically, becoming the school's diving champion. His academic results were not so good – though he did win a French prize. At the age of twelve he was sent to Salem school in Germany, run by Kurt Hahn. When Hahn, as a Jew, was forced to leave Germany, he founded Gordonstoun school in Scotland, and Philip followed him as a pupil.
'When Philip came to Gordonstoun his most marked trait was his undefeatable spirit. He felt the emotions of both joy and sadness very deeply, and the way he looked and moved indicated what he felt.' *Kurt Hahn*

At Gordonstoun Philip was given the part of Donalbain in the school's production of Macbeth, *not because of his acting talents but because:*
'There was nobody else who could be trusted to enter on horseback and not fall off.' *Prince Philip*

'A fair-haired boy, rather like a Viking with a sharp face and piercing blue eyes.' *Marion Crawford*

Philip's mother had returned to Greece, so he hardly ever saw her. His holidays were spent with other members of the family, particularly his mother's brother George (the Marquis of Milford Haven), who was like a second father to him. But in 1938 Uncle George died of cancer and his younger brother Dickie (Lord Mountbatten) now took charge of his young nephew. He had one year of Gordonstoun left before he had to decide what to do next. In his final year he became Guardian, or head boy.

'I don't think anybody thinks I had a father. Most people think that Dickie [Earl Mountbatten] is my father anyway.' *Prince Philip*

His final school report:

'Prince Philip is universally trusted, liked and respected. He has the greatest sense of service of all boys in the school. He is a born leader, but will need the exacting demands of a great service to do justice to himself. His best is outstanding; but his second best is not good enough. Prince Philip will make his mark in any profession but will have to prove himself in a full trial of strength.' *Kurt Hahn*

After Gordonstoun Philip entered the Royal Naval College at Dartmouth as a cadet. On 22 July 1939 he was told to look after the two little Princesses who had come with their parents to see the college. This was the moment that Princess Elizabeth was supposed to have fallen in love with him.

Sometime in 1941 his cousin Alexandra came across him writing a letter.
Alexandra: 'Who's it to?'
Philip: 'Lilibet. Princess Elizabeth in England.'
Alexandra: 'But she's only a baby!'
Philip: 'But perhaps I'm going to marry her.'

'He's very handsome. He has inherited the good looks of both sides of the family. He seems intelligent too. I should say he has plenty of common sense.' *Queen Mary*

THE ENGAGEMENT AND WEDDING

In the summer of 1946, Philip and Elizabeth were together at Balmoral and their thoughts turned towards marriage.
'It was probably then that we, that it became you know, that we began to think about it seriously, and even talk about it.' *Prince Philip*

Some time during August or September he proposed to her – but there is no record of what was said. Elizabeth, who had always been dutiful, accepted despite the fact that she did not have her parents' approval. However her parents were soon resigned to the fact that the couple were in love and intended to marry. They insisted that the engagement remain secret for the time being – but there were rumours. Once, when Elizabeth and Margaret were on an official visit this became clear:
Voice in the crowd: 'Where's Philip?'
Princess Margaret: 'Poor Lilibet. Nothing of your own. Not even your love affair.'

A statement from Buckingham Palace in September 1946 said there was no truth in the rumour that they were engaged and in February 1947 the young couple were parted when Elizabeth had to accompany her parents on a ten-week tour of South Africa. During the tour Elizabeth turned 21, and to mark the occasion made a broadcast to the Commonwealth.
'I declare before you all that my whole

life, whether it be long or short, shall be devoted to your service and the service of our great Imperial Commonwealth to which we all belong.' *Princess Elizabeth*

Two months after the return from South Africa, George VI allowed the engagement to be made official.
'It is with the greatest pleasure that The King and Queen announce the betrothal of their dearly beloved daughter, The Princess Elizabeth to Lieutenant Philip Mountbatten, RN, son of the late Prince Andrew of Greece and Princess Andrew (Princess Alice of Battenberg), to which union the King has gladly given his consent.'

'I am so glad you wrote and told Mummy that you think the long wait before your engagement and the long time before the wedding was for the best. I was rather afraid that you had thought I was being hard hearted about it.' *George VI*

'They both came to me after luncheon, looking radiant.' *Queen Mary*

Some time later Elizabeth visited Edinburgh.
'I am glad that at a time of great happiness I should find myself in Scotland. To me Scotland and happiness have always been closely interwoven.' *Princess Elizabeth*

Their first public appearance together was at a garden party at Buckingham Palace.
'I noticed that his uniform was shabby – it had the usual after-the-war look – and I liked him for not having got a new one for the occasion as many men would have done, to make an impression.' *Lady Airlie (family friend)*

Just before the wedding George VI created Philip a Royal Highness and gave him the titles of Duke of Edinburgh, Baron of Greenwich and Earl of Merioneth.
'A great deal to give a man all at once, but I know Philip understands his new responsibilities on his marriage to Lilibet.' *George VI*

The ceremony took place at Westminster Abbey.
'I was so proud of you and thrilled at

having you so close to me on our long walk in Westminster Abbey, but when I handed your hand to the Archbishop I felt that I had lost something very precious. You were so calm and composed during the Service and said your words with such conviction, that I knew it was all right.' *George VI*

'I can see that you are sublimely happy with Philip which is right but don't forget us is the wish of your ever loving and devoted PAPA.' *George VI*

'A week of gaiety such as the court has not seen for years. There were parties in St James's Palace to view the wedding presents, a royal dinner party for all the foreign Royalties, and an evening party at Buckingham Palace which seemed after the years of austerity like a scene out of a fairy tale.' *Queen Mary's lady-in-waiting*

After the wedding there was a request from the Board of Trade for her dress to go on tour to advertise British materials and workmanship.
'I can think of at least five reasons against.' *Princess Elizabeth*

'She thought that to do these things would be rather vulgarising the monarchy. It was her wedding dress. She didn't wish to part with it, or show it more openly than in St James's Palace, where it was displayed. It might seem to be advertising the expense that must have gone into such a dress. I think she felt there was something vulgar.' *Her private secretary*

The newly-weds moved into Clarence House, a novel experience for Philip:
'I've never really had a home. From the age of eight I've either been away at school or in the Navy.' *Prince Philip*

Elizabeth and Philip were married on 20 November 1947. On the morning of her wedding day she and Crawfie looked down at the waiting crowds.
'I can't believe it's really happening. I have to keep pinching myself.' *Princess Elizabeth*

—— THE YOUNG FAMILY ——

Why she chose the colour yellow for her forth-coming baby's cot and layette:
'Then no one can guess whether we want a boy or a girl. Fancy a poor little girl turning up and finding a blue-for-a-boy cot waiting for her!' *Princess Elizabeth*

'A boy and then a girl would be perfection!' *Princess Elizabeth*

Six days short of a year after the wedding, on 14 November 1948 Elizabeth and Philip's first child, Prince Charles was born.
'I still can't believe he is really mine, but perhaps that happens to new parents. Anyway this particular boy's parents couldn't be more proud of him.' *Princess Elizabeth*

On 15 August 1950, their second child, Princess Anne, was born. Elizabeth would take both her children out in the park, accompanied by her corgis.
'My corgis have become pram-minded. They pay more attention to the pram than me. They know it means a walk.' *Princess Elizabeth*

At the end of January 1952 Elizabeth and Philip set out on a tour of Australia and New Zealand. The King came to wave them off at the airport. It was the last time Elizabeth would see her father, for he died during the early hours of 6 February. Elizabeth was far away, on the top of a tree in Kenya when she became Queen. Philip was told first, and it was he who broke the news to his wife.
'He looked as if you'd dropped half the world on him. I never felt so sorry for anyone in all my life.' *Michael Parker (Prince Philip's Equerry)*

On becoming pregnant:
'We shall probably read about it in the papers before we really know ourselves.' *Princess Elizabeth*

Elizabeth became pregnant within three months of marriage.
'After all, it's what we're made for.' *Princess Elizabeth*

Waiting to greet them at Clarence House was Queen Mary.
'Her old Grannie and subject must be the first to kiss Her hand.' *Queen Mary*

Elizabeth's old nanny and confidante, Bobo McDonald, greeted the new Queen with a curtsey:
'Oh no, Bobo, *you* don't have to do that.' *The Queen*

'My heart is too full for me to say more to you today than that I shall always work as my father did.' *The Queen's accession declaration*

'I commend to you our dear daughter: give her your loyalty and devotion: in the great and lonely station to which she had been called she will need your protection and your love.' *The Queen Mother*

'I, whose youth was passed in the august, unchallenged and tranquil glare of the Victorian era, may well feel a thrill in invoking once more the prayer and anthem "God Save the Queen".' *Winston Churchill (Prime Minister)*

In July the Queen visited Edinburgh.
'It was a wonderful success. The Queen captured all hearts. She is certainly a real *Sovereign*, always doing the right thing instinctively. I only hope they will not kill the poor little girl with over-work.' *Queen Mary*

They travelled back to Britain immediately. A fleet of Royal limousines was waiting for the couple at the airport:
'Oh, they've sent those hearses.' *The Queen*

—— THE CORONATION ——

As the Coronation approached, the Queen found that she had developed a new confidence in her ability to handle her position.
'Extraordinary thing, I no longer feel anxious or worried – but I have lost all my timidity.' *The Queen*

On aspects of the Coronation ritual:
'Did my father do it? Then I will too.' *The Queen*

On whether to take a rest halfway through the ceremony:
'I'll be all right. I'm as strong as a horse.' *The Queen*

On Coronation morning, 2 June 1953, when it would be expected that the Queen would be feeling nervous about the day ahead, she was thinking of her favourite horse, Aureole, who was due to run in four days time.
Lady in waiting: 'All well, ma'am?'
The Queen: 'Oh, yes! The Captain has just rung up to say that Aureole went really well this morning!'

As the Queen was about to start the procession up Westminster Abbey, her heavy robes dragged along the thick carpet. She is known to have whispered a plea for help to the Archbishop of Canterbury.
'Get me started!' *The Queen*

In the autumn of 1956 Philip went on a tour of the Commonwealth, which lasted four months. His long absence started rumours that the marriage was on the rocks – and the Palace took the unprecedented step of making an announcement.

'It is quite untrue that there is any rift between the Queen and the Duke of Edinburgh.' *Sir Michael Adeane, press secretary*

'Those bloody lies that you people print to make money. These lies about how I'm never with my wife.' *Prince Philip*

Shortly after this the Queen confounded the gossips by making Philip a Prince of the United Kingdom (until then he had been Prince Philip of Greece, and a Royal Duke). In 1960 the Queen also took steps to correct the fact that Philip's surname was not taken by his children.

'While I and my children will continue to be styled and known as the House and Family of Windsor my descendents, other than descendants enjoying the style, title or attributes of Royal Highness and the titular dignity of Prince or Princess, and female descendants who marry and their descendants, shall bear the name Mountbatten-Windsor.' *The Queen*

The Queen made her first television broadcast in Canada in 1957. She was very nervous and tense, so Philip made her smile by reminding her of a private joke:
'Tell the Queen to remember the wailing and gnashing of teeth.' *Prince Philip*

About Charles and Anne, after Elizabeth and Philip returned from a long tour:
'I don't think they knew who we were.' *The Queen*

Prince Andrew was born on 19 February 1960.
'People want their first child very much. They want the second almost as much. If a third child comes along they accept it as natural, but they haven't gone out of their way to try and get it.' *Prince Philip*

'Dog leads cost money.' *The Queen*

'I sometimes feel like shooting the Queen's corgis.' *Princess Michael*

In 1961 the Queen was invited to Ghana as guest of President Nkrumah. The Prime Minister did not want her to accept because the President was in danger of being assassinated, and there were fears that the Queen might be killed or badly hurt if she travelled with him. But she insisted on going.
'If I were to cancel now Nkrumah might invite Khruschev instead and they wouldn't like that, would they?' *The Queen*

Prince Edward was born on 10 March 1964. Cecil Beaton took photographs of the baby.
'It's most unfortunate that all my sons have such long eyelashes while my daughter hasn't any at all.' *The Queen*

In the mini-skirt era, Princess Anne urged her mother to shorten her skirts.
'I am not a film star.' *The Queen*

In November 1972 the Queen and Prince Philip celebrated their Silver Wedding anniversary. The Queen's speech gave a rare flash of her privately notorious sense of humour:
'I think everyone will concede that on this day of all days I should begin with the words "My husband and I".' *The Queen*

In 1974 describing the British Police Force:
'Always overworked and sometimes undervalued, but never overpaid.' *The Queen*

In 1975, on his parents' marriage:
'I hope I will be as lucky as my parents, who have been so happy.' *Prince Charles*

In Jubilee year the Royal couple made a Commonwealth tour on the Royal Yacht Britannia, *during which they experienced a fierce gale.*
'Philip was not at all well . . . I'm glad to say.' *The Queen*

In 1977 Britain celebrated the Queen's 25 years on the throne with Silver Jubilee celebrations up and down the country. People queued all night in London for the Queen's walkabout, and were not put off by the rain. As she walked through the streets with Prince Philip the noise from the crowds was deafening.
'Do they always make a noise like that or is it something special today?' *Prince Philip*

In 1981 Prince Philip turned 60.
'I propose to work downhill gradually, grow old gracefully.' *Prince Philip*

On 13 June 1981 the Queen was shot at during the Trooping the Colour birthday parade. The gun contained only blanks, but this was not immediately known, and two members of her Household Cavalry spurred their horses forward to ride by her side, unsettling the Queen's horse further. Despite riding side-saddle she was able to calm her horse, and continue with the parade.
'It wasn't the shots that frightened her – but the Cavalry!' *The Queen*

But after it was over, she admitted to the problem of security:
'If someone wants to get me, it is too easy.' *The Queen*

Just over a year later on 12 July 1982, an intruder broke into Buckingham Palace and found his way to the Queen's bedroom. She remained cool and kept him talking for ten minutes until she was able to get help. Her chance came when he asked for a cigarette.
'You see I have none in this room. I will have some fetched for you.' *The Queen*

When the policemen finally arrived to arrest him:
'Oh come on! Get a bloody move on!' *The Queen*

To photographers on a state visit to Morocco, when the King of Morocco kept her waiting in a hot and airless tea tent:
'Keep your cameras trained; you may see the biggest walk-out of all time.' *The Queen*

To an ambassador, staring at a sandalled Franciscan monk at a reception:
'I am always fascinated by their toes, aren't you?' *The Queen*

Reported conversation between the Queen and a visitor in 1985, while Prince Andrew was in the Navy:
Visitor: 'You must miss Prince Andrew, Ma'am.'
The Queen: 'Indeed I do. Especially because he is the only one in the family who knows how to work the video.'
Visitor: 'Really – I should have thought Prince Philip would be able to do that.'
The Queen: 'In that case, you have clearly never flown with my husband.'

During her first and only visit to the Great Wall of China in 1986:
'Please take a picture, someone, or no one will believe I'm here.' *The Queen*

——— THE REAL QUEEN ———

'I am a traditionalist.' *The Queen*

'I have to be seen to be believed.' *The Queen*

'One can't really dance in a tiara.' *The Queen*

'The Queen rather likes things to go a bit wrong – then she copes.' *A lady-in-waiting*

'I have been trained since childhood never to show emotion in public.' *The Queen*

Describing the diary she has kept since she was a child:
'My secret friend.' *The Queen*

'A marvellous person and a wonderful mother. Terribly sensible and wise.'
Prince Charles

'A good gossip is a wonderful tonic.'
The Queen

'I'm the first Queen who's ever been able to drive!' *The Queen*

'I have no time to read large books now, only small ones.' *The Queen*

'Andrew's mother particularly enjoys Ken Bruce and Derek Jameson. She doesn't like the Radio Four "Today" programme because she says she has read all the serious stuff in the newspapers.' *The Duchess of York*

In a village shop in Sandringham:
Fellow shopper: 'Excuse me, but you do look like the Queen.'
The Queen (smiling): 'How very reassuring.'

'If it weren't for my Archbishop of Canterbury, I should be off in my plane to Longchamps every Sunday.'
The Queen

Having watched Prince Philip drink three champagne cocktails at a reception
'What kind of speech do you think you are going to make now?' *The Queen*

To Prince Philip, seeing him eating snails:
'However can you eat those beastly things?' *The Queen*

Declining a 1930s-style hat suggested by her milliner, Frederick Fox in 1988:
'Have we been watching too much "Edward and Mrs Simpson", do you think Mr Fox?' *The Queen*

Telling Susan Crosland, wife of Anthony Crosland, then Foreign Secretary, how to stand for hours without getting tired:
'One plants one's feet apart like this [hoisting long skirt above her ankles to demonstrate]. Always keep them parallel. Make sure your weight is evenly distributed. That's all there is to it.' *The Queen*

'I am used to standing. I have been standing all my life. *The Queen*

The Queen Mother: 'I'm going to live to be a hundred.'
The Queen: 'Then it will be Charles who'll send you your centenarian telegram.'

'I love looking at houses, but I never get the chance. It would be too awkward to invite myself in. My husband heard me talking about this one day and ever since then, if we are in the car and we pass by a nice house, he drives up to it to have a look. I get terribly embarrassed sometimes and all I can do is duck down and hide.' *The Queen*

'It's extraordinary. My mother doesn't need glasses at all and here I am 52 – 56 – well, whatever age I am, and can't see a thing.' *The Queen*

On being told that the office of a left-wing privy councillor was in the run-down area of the Elephant and Castle in London:
'Oh, what a with-it address.' *The Queen*

To a ballet dancer at a Palace luncheon:
'I'm amazed you manage to remember all the steps. Everyone must be absolutely puffed at the end of half an hour. I know I should be.' *The Queen*

To photographer Vic Blackman who accidentally grabbed her to keep his balance during a crowd surge:
'Not your fault, Mr Blackman. It will give you something to write about if you ever write your memoirs.' *The Queen*

During a visit to an artifical insemination unit for livestock, the Queen asked her host for the identity of an object she did not know. When told it was a vagina, she replied:
'Ask a silly question . . .' *The Queen*

President Reagan's verdict on the Queen:
'Down to earth.'

'Don't ask me to explain why it is that the Queen has an official birthday in June, when her proper birthday is in April. You'll just have to accept it like cricket, pounds, shillings and pence and other quaint but quite practical British customs.' *Prince Philip*

Lady Diane Cooper was chatting to a 'nice little woman' at Sir Robert Mayer's 100th birthday celebrations, when she realised that it was the Queen.
Lady Diana Cooper: 'Oh, ma'am. Please, ma'am. I'm so sorry, ma'am — I didn't recognise you without your crown.'
The Queen (pleasantly dismissing the gaffe): 'I thought it was Sir Robert's night, not mine!'

After a luncheon guest, while waiting to be served with his asparagus, had watched the Queen eating hers:
'Now it's my turn to see *you* make a pig of yourself!' *The Queen*

To the wives of miners:
'I find it difficult keeping my floors clean too.' *The Queen*

THE QUEEN'S ROLE

'Because she's the Sovereign everyone turns to her. If you have a King and a Queen, there are certain things people automatically go to the Queen about. But if the Queen is also the *Queen*, they go to her about everything. She's asked to do much more than she would normally do.' *Prince Philip*

'She does *not* enjoy "society". She likes her horses. But she loves her duty and means to be a queen and not a puppet.' *Harold Macmillan (Prime Minister)*

'I do not think anyone fully realises the accumulation of experience she has.' *Margaret Thatcher (Prime Minister)*

Mrs Thatcher was embarrassed when, at a public ceremony, she and the Queen appeared in similar outfits. Mrs Thatcher sent a memo to the Palace asking if she could know beforehand what the Queen would be wearing on such occasions. The reply came back as follows:
'Do not worry. The Queen does not notice what other people are wearing.'

'I simply ache with smiling . . . The trouble is that women are expected to be smiling all the time. If a man looks solemn it is automatically assumed he is a serious person, concentrating, with grave things on his mind.' *The Queen*

On the Queen's relationship with her prime ministers:
'What one gets is friendliness not friendship.' *James Callaghan (Prime Minister)*

Her favourite Prime Minister
'Winston, of course, because it was always such fun.' *The Queen*

When Winston Churchill retired in the sixties, he was asked:
'Do you want a dukedom or anything like that?' *The Queen*

When an MP remarked that it must be a strain for her to meet so many strangers:
'It is not as difficult as it might seem. You see, I don't have to introduce myself. They all seem to know who I am.' *The Queen*

Asked by a student if she had a mechanical arm inside her coat to help with all the waving:
'Oh no. I haven't reached that stage yet.' *The Queen*

To Ronald Ferguson, the Duchess of York's father, in 1964 when, as her equerry, he rode too close to her coach during a procession:
'Back a bit, Ron – they've come to see me, not you!' *The Queen*

To an ambassador who used several complex psychiatric terms to describe an erratic Eastern politician:
'What are you really saying is that he is bonkers.' *The Queen*

Conversation in 1965, reported by Lord Mountbatten:
The Queen: 'It might be wise to abdicate at a time when Charles could do better.'
Prince Philip: 'You might be right. The doctors will keep you alive so long.'

Arriving in the pouring rain on her US tour in 1983:
'I knew before we came that we had exported many of our traditions to the United States. I had not realised before that the weather was one of them.' *The Queen*

Describing how she once had to raise a sword high to enoble a very tall man:
'I heard a ripping noise and my sleeve got torn. It was hard to know who was the most embarrassed.' *The Queen*

Would the Queen ever agree to be interviewed?
'I think, probably, the risks would be greater than the benefits.' *Prince Philip*

When it was suggested that there may be a British Republic one day:
'We'll go quietly.' *The Queen*

THE REAL PRINCE PHILIP

Catching her husband playing with an electric train:
The Queen: 'I thought that belonged to Charles.'
Prince Philip: 'Oh I look after it for him while he's at school.'

'I don't like to be "Highnessed". Just call me "Sir". This is the twentieth century.' *Prince Philip*

To a footman who tried to open a door for him:
'I've got hands. I can open a door myself.' *Prince Philip*

Is he a male chauvinist?
'I'd find it difficult in my position.' *Prince Philip*

Describing himself:
'An uncultured polo-playing clot . . . I'm one of those stupid bums who never went to university . . . and I don't think it's done me any harm.' *Prince Philip*

'A discredited Balkan prince of no particular merit or distinction.' *Prince Philip*

On the fact that his children were not to take his surname, but the name of Windsor (changed later so that they took the name Mountbatten-Windsor):
'It makes me an amoeba – a bloody amoeba!' *Prince Philip*

'I'm one of the most governed people you could hope to meet – almost permanently under arrest.' *Prince Philip*

'Never cancel an engagement. If you have a headache, take an aspirin.' *Prince Philip*

'The trouble is that I'm spoilt – everything's nearly always right, so the odd occasion when they go wrong is more noticeable. I get just as angry with myself if I make a mistake or do something wrong.' *Prince Philip*

'Without the chance of receiving the message of religious thought, the most well-meaning, energetic and intelligent human is really no more than a bumble-bee trapped in a bottle.' *Prince Philip*

Does he miss being able to walk unnoticed in a public park?
'It's like saying don't you miss going to the moon. I mean, I just haven't the opportunity of going to the moon . . . You can't go through life desperately wanting to be somebody else, wanting to do something else all the time.' *Prince Philip*

What would he like to be remembered for?
'I doubt I've achieved anything likely to be remembered.' *Prince Philip*

About sport:
'Ten minutes' doing is worth ten hours' watching.' *Prince Philip*

About polo:
'Wives play an extremely important part in polo and many promising young players have had the terrible choice of keeping their ponies or keeping their wife.' *Prince Philip*

'Philip's a born boss, but he does it nicely.' *Princess Margaret*

'I am always wary of sticking my nose into things which do not directly concern me.' *Prince Philip*

PRINCE PHILIP'S ROLE

'Inevitably it's an awkward situation to be in. There's only one other person really like me – Prince Bernhard of the Netherlands. He's the only other member of the union, so to speak.' *Prince Philip*

'It's almost like being self-employed in the sense that you decide what to do.' *Prince Philip*

On a trip to Canada in 1969:
'We don't come here for our health. We can think of better ways of enjoying ourselves.' *Prince Philip*

In Vancouver:
'I declare this thing open whatever it is.' *Prince Philip*

When offered a stetson hat on the tour:
'What? Not another one.' *Prince Philip It was then explained to the Prince that the stetson was a symbol of Canadian hospitality.*
'Oh well, I suppose I can always turn it into a flower pot.' *Prince Philip*

On being asked to define protocol:
'If you don't know, you're a very lucky man.' *Prince Philip*

Overheard whispering to his wife at an official function:
'Cheer up sweetie, give them a smile.' *Prince Philip*

'Constitutionally I don't exist.' *Prince Philip*

PRINCE PHILIP ON ROYALTY

'What you want is a dynasty production where everyone can see what we do privately. But the point is people only want to know the splashy things, or the scandalous things. They're not really interested in anything else.' *Prince Philip*

About the Queen's Christmas television broadcast:
'Television is a difficult medium through which to deliver this kind of message. In the old days, when it was just a spoken message, people turned on the wireless and it was fine. But somehow, it's not the same to have the Queen looking into a television camera. It's hard to know how we can get over this. Perhaps the alternative is to dress it up and call it "the Queen's show".' *Prince Philip*

'It is a complete misconception to imagine that the monarchy exists in the interests of the Monarch. It doesn't. It exists in the interests of the people.' *Prince Philip*

To the dictator of Paraguay, Alfredo Stroessner, on an official tour in 1969:
'It's a pleasant change to be in a country that isn't ruled by its people.' *Prince Philip*

Royal children:
'We try to keep our children out of the public eye so that they can grow up as normally as possible. But if you are really going to have a monarchy, you have got to have a family and the family's got to be in the public eye.' *Prince Philip*

'Monarchy involves the whole family, which means that different age groups are part of it. There are people who can look, for instance, at the Queen Mother and identify with that generation, or with us, or with our children.' *Prince Philip*

When will Charles succeed to the throne?:
'Are you asking me when the Queen is going to die?' *Prince Philip*

THE OUTSPOKEN PRINCE

'You must sometimes stretch out your neck, but not actually give them the axe.' *Prince Philip*

'There's an awful lot of things that, if I were to re-read them now, I'd say to myself: "Good God, I wish I hadn't said that".' *Prince Philip*

'The idea that you don't do anything on the off chance you might be criticised, you'd end up like a cabbage and it's pointless. You've got to stick up for something you believe in.' *Prince Philip*

'Sacred cows thrive on being taken seriously; they cannot stand being laughed at.' *Prince Philip*

On seeing the mayor and councillors of Nottingham approaching to welcome him during an official visit to the town:
'Here comes the chain gang.' *Prince Philip*

'Always try and break the ice with a joke; even if it's not a very good one, they will know you are trying to put them at ease.' *Prince Philip*

'I find myself in the delightful position of telling people who know much more about it, what they ought to do, in the certain knowledge that I will not have to attempt to do what I suggest.' *Prince Philip*

During a session with photographer Cecil Beaton:
'Surely we've had enough. If he's not got what he wants by now he's an even worse photographer than I think he is.' *Prince Philip*

'I'm sick and tired of making excuses for Britain.' *Prince Philip*

'Third World? Why does everyone go on about it? What I want to know is where is the Second World?' *Prince Philip*

'The man who invented the red carpet ought to have his head examined.' *Prince Philip*

'How does a girl get a mink? The same way a mink gets a mink.' *Prince Philip*

Definition of a horse:
'The biggest animal with the smallest brain.' *Prince Philip*

'Parting with money in the aid of a good cause is always painful.' *Prince Philip*

On drugs:
'It is not really a question of whether they are legal or illegal, but whether it is sensible or not.' *Prince Philip*

When told that London Transport was to name its new line the Jubilee Line:
'Does that mean there will be 25-year intervals between trains?' *Prince Philip*

'Marriage gains from the web of family relationships between parents and children, grandparents and grandchildren, cousins, aunts and uncles.' *The Queen*

MARRIAGE AND FAMILY LIFE

On family life:
'I am for it.' *The Queen*

'In my view, one should tax people on the number of people they have.' *Prince Philip*

When it was pointed out that this would mean only the rich could have large families:
'Damn good thing.' *Prince Philip*

Queen Juliana of the Netherlands: 'What do you do when your husband wants something and you don't want him to have it?'
The Queen: 'Oh, I just tell him he shall have it and then make sure he doesn't get it.'

'Woman's paramount duty is the home. It's there she finds her truest fulfilment.' *The Queen*

'When a man opens a car door for his wife, it's either a new car or a new wife.' *Prince Philip*

'Only a moral imperative can persuade husbands and wives to be faithful to each other.' *Prince Philip*

On Royal children:
'Public life is not a fair burden to place upon them.' *The Queen*

'The children soon discover that it's much safer to unburden yourself to a member of the family than just a friend . . . You see, you're never quite sure . . . a small indiscretion can lead to all sorts of difficulties.' *Prince Philip*

'I've always tried to help them master at least one thing, because as soon as a child feels self-confidence in one area, it spills over into all others . . . this is immediately reflected even in their academic performance.' *Prince Philip*

—— ROYAL RESIDENCES ——

'They say an Englishman's home is his castle. What I want is to turn my castle into a home.' *The Queen*

'I know all about noise. I live at the end of an airport runway.' *The Queen*

The Queen: 'I wish I could live here for ever and ever.'
Princess Margaret: 'You'd soon be bored.'
The Queen: 'Oh no! Nobody could possibly be bored at Windsor!'

Sandringham:
'Sandringham is so dear to me because it means so much to my husband.' *The Queen*

Buckingham Palace:
'Living there is like living over the shop.' *Prince Philip*

About the gold plates used for state dinners:
'At least they don't break if you drop them.' *Prince Philip*

To a footman who apologised after tepid food was served during a banquet:
"Don't worry. People come here not for hot food but to eat off gold plate.' *The Queen*

The Royal Mews:
'It's a village in itself . . . It's a community more than anything else – the horses and the people who look after them, and it's like a small village which you know belongs to Buckingham Palace.' *The Queen*

On flying:
Official: 'How was your flight, Sir?'
Prince Philip: 'Have you ever flown?'
Official: 'Yes Sir.'
Prince Philip: 'Well, it was like that.'

'I fly because it's useful for getting about, but I also enjoy the . . . intellectual challenge of it all, if that's the right word.' *Prince Philip*

On architecture:
'You design an engine according to a certain mechanical law – the same is true of planning for a community. If you do it right you get a happy and satisfied community; if you do it wrong you get all the well-known social diseases.' *Prince Philip*

'People should take a more careful look around them, and not just accept the mess in the streets and the mess on the skyline.' *Prince Philip*

On the environment:
'Modern human civilisation needs new resources but there is one very important proviso – that permanent, irreversible or unacceptable levels of environmental damage must not be allowed.' *Prince Philip*

On lavatories:
'The biggest waste of water in the country by far. You spend half a pint and flush two gallons.' *Prince Philip*

'The older I get the more cynical I get in the sense that I just think things are going to get worse. I have nightmares about the world the next generation, or the generation after that, is going to live in.' *Prince Philip*

'You can be forgiven for coming to the conclusion that the world is rapidly going to pot.' *Prince Philip*

On hunting:
'I don't see the difference between eating wild animals killed by myself and domestic animals killed by a professional in an abattoir. I shoot the surplus of a wild population and make sure that I leave enough to breed another surplus next year. This may be a moral issue for some. It is certainly not a conservation issue. The danger is in taking more than can be replaced. This applies to fish in the sea and trees in the forest.' *Prince Philip*

To an anti-hunting lobbyist who admitted to eating meat:
'It's like saying adultery is all right as long as you don't enjoy it.' *Prince Philip*

'They're just people who wait around for the moment when you pick your nose to take a photograph of you.'
Prince Philip

PRINCE PHILIP ON THE PRESS

Proposing the toast for a newspaper charity:
'I'm in a bit of a quandary this evening because I can't very well talk about charity all the time . . . In which case I'm left with the press and, quite frankly, I'd rather be left with a baby.'
Prince Philip

When a photographer fell out of a tree in India:
'I hope he breaks his bloody neck.'
Prince Philip

To the people of Dominica:
'You have mosquitoes, we have the press.' *Prince Philip*

'There are times when I would very much like to be a newspaper owner.'
Prince Philip

3

PRINCESS MARGARET

&

HER FAMILY

── PRINCESS MARGARET ──

Princess Margaret Rose was born on 21 August 1930 at Glamis Castle. The second daughter of the Duke and Duchess of York, her elder sister Princess 'Lilibet' Elizabeth was four years old. At the time of her birth Margaret was fourth in line to the throne and, as was the custom in those days, the Home Secretary, Mr Clynes and Harry Boyd, the Ceremonial Secretary, had to be present at the birth. Concerned that they might miss the crucial moment, the two men turned up seventeen days early, on 4 August.

'I feel so sorry for Mr Clynes having to wait so long. I always wanted him to come up when he was sent for, which would have been so much simpler.' *George VI, when Duke of York.*

'E. looking very well and the baby a darling.' *Queen Mary*

The new mother wanted to call her baby Ann

On being told that despite being dressed as an angel for a fancy dress party she didn't look very angelic:
'That's all right. I'll be a holy terror.'
Princess Margaret

Margaret, and told the King and Queen.
'I think Ann of York sounds pretty, and Elizabeth and Ann go so well together. I wonder what you think? Lots of people have suggested Margaret, but it has no family links really on either side.' *The Queen Mother, when Duchess of York.*

The King did not approve of the name Ann, so the baby was christened Margaret Rose instead.
'You gave Lilibet three names. Why didn't you give *me* three instead of only two? Margaret Rose!' *Princess Margaret, aged about ten.*

Lady Strathmore, Margaret's maternal grandmother, was carrying the nine-month-old Margaret downstairs when the baby started to hum correctly the waltz from The Merry Widow.
'I was so astounded that I almost dropped her.' *Lady Strathmore.*

Sir James Barrie, creator of Peter Pan, and a family friend, attended Margaret's fifth birthday party.
'Some of her presents were on the table, simple things that might have come from the sixpenny shops, but she was in a frenzy of glee over them, especially one to which she had given the place of honour by her plate. I said to her as one astounded, "Is that really your very own?" and she saw how I envied and immediately placed it between us with the words, "It is yours and mine".' *Sir James Barrie*

At another party when she was six Margaret prayed the conjurer would not call her up on the stage – and he didn't.
'That childish experience gave me confidence in the power of prayer, which I've believed in ever since.' *Princess Margaret*

On the fact that Elizabeth was always better behaved:
'Isn't it lucky that Lilibet's the eldest?' *Princess Margaret*

Margaret had two imaginary friends when she was small, 'Cousin Halifax' and 'Inderbombanks'. She invented them because she and Elizabeth spent most of their time together alone. They were very different: Elizabeth was good and controlled, whereas Margaret was difficult, with a wicked sense of humour. When Margaret was told off by her nanny for being naughty, she would blame her imaginary partner in crime.
'It wasn't me, it was Cousin Halifax.' *Princess Margaret*

Sisterly rivalry:
'Margaret always wants what I want!' *Princess Elizabeth*

When assured that nothing was impossible if you tried hard enough:
'Have you ever tried putting toothpaste back into its tube?' *Princess Margaret*

About visits to art galleries when a child:
'When I grew up I decided my children should never be allowed to see more than three great pictures at a time, so that they would actually plead for "just one more", instead of dropping with fatigue.' *Princess Margaret*

On being told of the death of her grandfather, George V, when she was six:
'Grandpa has gone to heaven and I am sure God is finding him very useful.' *Princess Margaret*

After King Edward VIII abdicated in 1936, Margaret's father became King, and she was now second in line to the throne. What bothered the little six-year-old most was that she had just learnt how to write her name, and now it was wrong:
'I used to be Margaret of York and now I'm nothing.' *Princess Margaret*

When told her father would be King:
'Will you have to sing "God Save My Gracious Me"?' *Princess Margaret*

Whether Margaret should attend the Coronation:
'She is a bit young for a Coronation, isn't she?' *Princess Elizabeth*

When war broke out the Princesses were evacuated to Windsor:
'Who *is* this Hitler spoiling everything?' *Princess Margaret*

'There was a tremendous spirit at Windsor. Everybody was always cheerful.' *Princess Margaret*

'We were not allowed to go far from the house in case there were air-raids; and there had been a pathetic attempt to defend the castle with trenches and some rather feeble barbed wire. It could not have kept anyone out, but it did keep us in.' *Princess Margaret*

Margaret's first appearance on radio was in October 1940, on Children's Hour, *when Elizabeth was making a broadcast to the nation's children. She ended with the words, 'My sister is by my side, and we are both going to say goodnight to you. Come on, Margaret.'*
'Good night and good luck to you all.' *Princess Margaret*

'Espiègle' (little rogue). *Queen Mary*

To a very fat visitor, while prodding him in the stomach:
'Is that *all* of you?' *Princess Margaret*

Of her high soprano voice:
'I was able to hit F above high C.' *Princess Margaret*

Verdict on Princess Margaret:
'So outrageously amusing that one can't help encouraging her.' *Queen Mary*

Letter to her governess, Crawfie, in 1943:
'As you never write to me, I'm going to write to you. Ha! Ha! How are you? Did you have a happy Xmas! We did. Philip came! On Xmas Eve we all had dinner together. There were only nine of us . . . Then after dinner, we put out all the lights and listened to a GHOST STORY. We settled ourselves to be frightened – and were NOT. Most disappointing. Then we danced (on the little bits of board we could find) to the wireless as the gramophone wouldn't work.

'Then on Xmas night we had dinner together. The Bofors officers came. Quite nice. Then we rolled back the carpet and danced to the gramophone as it had been mended. Danced till *one o'clock*! . . .

'Lilibet has a cold. BOTHER . . . With heaps, piles, mounds, mountains of love from Margaret.'

It was about this time that she first met Peter Townsend, her father's equerry.
'My father became very fond of Peter. They both stammered and that was a bond. When he first appeared, I had a terrific crush on him. But there was no question of romance until much later – he was a married man.' *Princess Margaret*

In 1947 Elizabeth married Philip, and Margaret was now on her own. She made friends with Sharman Douglas, the American Ambassador's daughter, and started to hang around with the lively group of people Sharman knew. Margaret by now was very beautiful, and attracting a lot of press attention. All the movements of the so-called 'Margaret Set' were documented in the society pages.
'Most of the people who became my friends – and they generally had other and much closer friends of their own – were Sharman's friends first. So if anything, it was *her* set, not mine. There never was a "Margaret Set".' *Princess Margaret*

When she was reprimanded by her sister for flirting outrageously with some navy cadets:
'Look after your Empire and I'll look after my life.' *Princess Margaret*

Margaret's social life became a whirl of restaurants and clubs, far more sophisticated than Elizabeth's. There were a lot of eligible young men in this set with whom her name became linked.

'Girls of one's own age were not really interested in what one did officially, but one's men friends were polite enough to listen.' *Princess Margaret*

On 5 February 1952 Margaret's beloved father died. Her mother was in deep mourning and her sister was busy with her new role as Queen, as well as with her young family. For comfort Margaret turned to her father's former equerry and current Comptroller to the Queen Mother's Household, Group Captain Peter Townsend, who had recently divorced his wife on the grounds of her adultery. Margaret had been in love with Townsend for some time, but it was in the summer of 1952 that he began to feel the same for her. The problem was that the Queen's consent had to be given, and marriage to a divorced man was against the teachings of the Church. The couple told the Queen and the Queen Mother in the spring of 1953.

'If disconcerted, as they had every reason to be, they did not flinch, but faced it with perfect calm and, it must be said, considerable charity.' *Group Captain Peter Townsend*

Although the Queen was happy for them, and would in other circumstances have been pleased for them to marry, she was head of the Church of England and this had to influence her decisions.

'Under the circumstances it isn't unreasonable for me to ask you to wait a year.' *The Queen*

Townsend took the problem to the Queen's Private Secretary, Sir Alan Lascelles.
'You must be either mad or bad.' *Sir Alan Lascelles*

At this stage no one said that the marriage was out of the question.
'Had he said we *couldn't* get married we wouldn't have thought any more about it. But nobody bothered to explain anything to us.' *Princess Margaret*

Townsend was removed from the Queen Mother's Household to become one of the Queen's equerries. The British press had printed nothing about the romance (although there had been speculation abroad) until the Coronation on 2 June 1953, when a small but intimate gesture alerted the assembled reporters:

'A great crowd of crowned heads, of nobles and commons – and newspapermen, British and foreign – were gathered in the Great Hall. Princess Margaret came up to me; she looked superb, sparkling, ravishing. As we chatted she brushed a bit of fluff off my uniform. We laughed and thought no more of it.' *Group Captain Peter Townsend*

The story was in all the papers. The Prime Minister told the Queen that the Cabinet were unanimously against the marriage and so were the Commonwealth prime ministers. The only way that Margaret could marry would be to renounce her right of succession to the throne. Shortly after this Margaret accompanied the Queen Mother on a trip to Rhodesia, and while they were away Townsend was posted to Brussels. The couple had been asked to wait for another year, but when that was up the Government were still against the marriage. In October 1955 Margaret and Townsend met to talk about it.

'We were both exhausted, mentally, emotionally, physically. We felt mute and numbed at the centre of this maelstrom.' *Group Captain Peter Townsend*

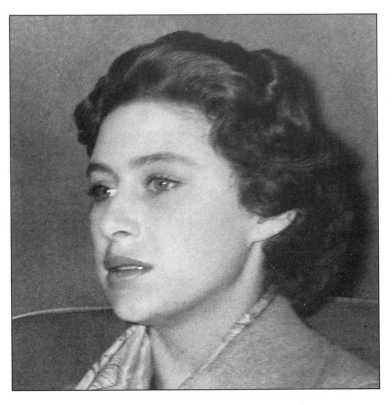

The statement that Margaret and Townsend had drafted together was released on 31 October 1955.

'I would like it to be known that I have decided not to marry Group Captain Peter Townsend. I have been been aware that, subject to my renouncing my rights of succession, it might have been possible for me to contract a civil marriage. But mindful of the Church's teachings that Christian marriage is indissoluble, and conscious of my duty to the Commonwealth, I have resolved to put these considerations before others. I have reached this decision entirely alone and in doing so I have been strengthened by the unfailing support and devotion of Group Captain Peter Townsend. I am deeply grateful for the concern of all those who have constantly prayed for my happiness.' *Princess Margaret*

They had decided that marriage was impossible and together they worked out the statement which would explain her feelings.

'For a few moments we looked at each other; there was a wonderful tenderness in her eyes which reflected, I suppose, the look in mine. We had reached the end of the road.' *Group Captain Peter Townsend*

Margaret felt it was important to tell the Archbishop of Canterbury of her decision. When she went to see him he was in the act of reaching for a book, which she supposed he wanted to quote from to help her.

'You can put away your books Archbishop. I am not going to marry Peter Townsend. I wanted you to know first.' *Princess Margaret*

'She could have married me only if she'd been prepared to give up everything. I simply hadn't the weight, I knew it, to counterbalance all she would have lost. Thinking of it calmly . . . you couldn't have expected her to become an ordinary housewife overnight, could you? And to be fair, I wouldn't have wanted that for her.' *Group Captain Peter Townsend*

On 20 February 1958 Margaret met the photographer Antony Armstrong-Jones at a dinner party, where they were both guests of Lady Elizabeth Cavendish. Margaret was told that Tony was a bohemian.
Princess Margaret: 'What *is* a bohemian? What does it mean?'
Lady-in-waiting: 'Well, Ma'am, it means he won't always turn up to lunch when he says he will.'

Antony Armstrong-Jones was born in London on 7 March 1030. His father was the barrister Ronald Armstrong-Jones, his mother Anne (née Messel), whose brother was Oliver Messel the theatrical designer. Tony's parents divorced when he was four; his father married twice more, and his mother once more, to the Earl of Rosse.

Tony's first school was Sandroyd preparatory, followed by Eton; he was not very academic.
'Maybe he is interested in some subject, but it isn't a subject we teach here.' *Report by one of Tony's teachers*

He had his first photography lessons from a local chemist, and while still at school attempted to get some photographs published in The Tatler, *but was put off by the commissionaire at the door.*
'I was too frightened to go there again and never dared to meet any of the people.' *Antony Armstrong-Jones*

As a teenager Tony contracted polio and spent more than a year in a wheelchair. The illness left him with one leg shorter than the other. He later went to Cambridge to study Architecture. While there he coxed for Cambridge Eight rowing team, and continued to practise his photography. His studies suffered, and he wrote to his mother saying that he wanted to be a photographer rather than an architect.
'Do not agree suggestion changing career.' *Telegram from Lady Rosse*

Tony, unsurprisingly, came down from university without a degree.
'Failed quite brilliantly.'
Antony Armstrong-Jones

Tony then set about becoming a photographer. He became apprenticed to Baron, a society photographer, and six months later set up on his own with the help of a thousand pounds from his father. He soon became successful as a theatrical and society photographer, and was asked to take photographs of the young Prince Charles and Princess Anne. The Queen liked them so much that she asked him to take some pictures of her. But curiously he had never met Margaret before that dinner party.

Prince Philip gave Margaret away, and walked her up the aisle to the waiting groom.
Prince Philip: 'Am I holding on to you, or are you holding on to me?'
Princess Margaret: 'I'm holding on to you.'
Prince Philip: 'I don't know who's more nervous, you or me.'

THE ENGAGEMENT
──── AND MARRIAGE ────

Tony lived in Pimlico, but also rented a room in a terraced house in London's Dockland, decades before it became fashionable. As his friendship with Margaret progressed, this was where he invited her to visit him.

'It had the most marvellous view. One walked into the room and there was the river straight in front. At high tide swans looked in. And because it was on a bend of the river you looked towards the Tower and Tower Bridge with the dome of St Paul's behind them to the left, and the docks to the right.' *Princess Margaret*

The fact that Tony was already well known as a royal photographer was a good screen for the developing romance. The press had no idea about it at all, and nothing was made of the fact that Tony's name was regularly among the people who partied with Margaret. In 1959 Tony took the official photographs to mark Margaret's 29th birthday. Later, meeting Cecil Beaton who usually photographed her, Margaret said, 'I've been faithless to you.' He later wrote:

'I knew at once that she had had her photograph taken by T A-J. This was a blow, but I thought it extremely honest and frank to tell me before the pictures appeared. I showed great tact by muttering, "I'm so glad . He's such a nice young man and deserves his success. If I have to have a rival, I'm glad it's him and not Baron." ' *Cecil Beaton*

Shortly afterwards the Queen invited Tony to stay at Balmoral, and the family approved of him. A few weeks later Townsend wrote to Margaret telling her that he had fallen in love with a girl he planned to marry. Marga-

ret told Tony about the letter, which had shocked her – but asked him not to propose to her himself.

'He eventually did, but in a roundabout way. It was very cleverly worded.' *Princess Margaret*

They became privately engaged in December 1959.
The Queen Mother: 'I'm *so* pleased you are going to marry Margaret.'
Antony Armstrong-Jones: 'Ssh! I haven't asked the Queen yet!'

Once the Queen was asked she was only too pleased to agree, and the official announcement was made on 26 February 1960.
'It is with the greatest pleasure that Queen Elizabeth the Queen Mother announces the betrothal of her beloved daughter The Princess Margaret to Mr Antony Charles Robert Armstrong-Jones, son of Mr R O L Armstrong-Jones QC, and the Countess of Rosse, to which union the Queen has gladly given her consent.'

Other members of the family were less happy.
'Lunched with the Duchess [of Kent, Princess Marina] and Princess Alexandra. They are *not* pleased over Princess Margaret's engagement. There was a distinct *froideur* when I mentioned it.' *Noel Coward*

They were married on 6 May 1960 in Westminster Abbey. It was the first royal wedding to be televised live.
'It meant that those of my friends who couldn't come could still see it. I loved that idea.' *Princess Margaret*

At one point when repeating her vows, Princess Margaret anticipated the Archbishop of Canterbury.
'I knew the words so well. I'd practised them over and over, so that

instead of repeating "From this day forward" I beat the Archbishop to the next line, "For better, for worse".' *Princess Margaret*

The honeymoon was a six-week cruise of the Caribbean, during which Margaret saw Mustique for the first time.
'When I knew Princess Margaret was getting married I asked her if she would like a present in a box or a plot of land on Mustique. She chose the land.' *Colin Tennant, family friend*

On their return they moved into 10 Kensington Palace.
'A doll's house.' *Princess Margaret*

At first Tony gave up his career to act as consort to his wife, but this made him unhappy.
'It was like a pilot sacrificing his career for his marriage . . . but watching every plane with the thought, "I should be up there." ' *Jocelyn Stevens, family friend*

Cautiously Tony began to work again, first by joining the Council of Industrial Design in an advisory capacity, and then designing a new aviary for London Zoo. When it became known that Princess Margaret was pregnant and due to have a baby in November 1961 Tony was offered an Earldom so that their children would have titles. He chose to be known as the first Earl of Snowdon, Viscount Linley of Nymans. On 3 November 1961 their son David Albert Charles was born, and was given the title Viscount Linley.
'The Princess and I are absolutely thrilled and delighted.' *Lord Snowdon*

Tony was offered the job of artistic adviser on The Sunday Times *and his appoint-*

ment was announced in January 1962. Later that year the Snowdons moved into the larger apartments of 1A Kensington Palace, where Princess Margaret still lives. On 1 May 1964 Margaret gave birth to a daughter at Kensington Palace. Margaret and Tony planted a climbing rose in their garden to commemorate the baby's birth. Ten weeks later on 13 July she was christened Sarah Frances Elizabeth. At the end of August that year the Snowdons went on holiday with some friends.

'I called Princess Margaret "the Master Planner". She loved planning what we were going to do and keeps the most marvellous albums which she faithfully writes up . . . She loved it. It was the most *marvellous* holiday and she and Tony got on so well.' *Jocelyn Stevens*

But the marriage was already starting to go wrong. Tony was becoming increasingly involved with his work, and less happy to be a constant consort to his wife. Margaret was unhappy, but tried not to show it. In February 1967, while Tony was once more travelling for work, reports of the marriage being on the rocks reached the newspapers. Tony made a public statement:

'Nothing has happened to our marriage. When I am away – and I'm away quite a lot on assignments for my paper – I write home and I telephone like other husbands in love with their wives. I telephoned today. I can't understand what started this, but some of these papers have been hinting about this since six months after my marriage. No responsible journalist could possibly take seriously such silly stories.' *Lord Snowdon*

'He never rang or wrote when he was abroad, which made it awkward when friends asked for news of him.' *Princess Margaret*

THE BREAK-UP

Tony continued to be liked and valued by the rest of the Royal Family. In 1969, as Constable of Caenarvon Castle, he was designer-in-chief of Prince Charles's Investiture as Prince of Wales. In May 1973 the Snowdons spent their last holiday together as a family, and after that led very separate lives. In September of that year Princess Margaret met Roddy Llewellyn, a man sixteen years her junior, with whom she became very close friends. Their friendship was eventually to make Roddy notorious.

'I would much rather have been remembered for having painted a marvellous picture.' *Roddy Llewellyn*

In 1974, while Roddy went on an extended holiday, Margaret had a nervous breakdown.

At one point she took too many sleeping pills, and it was said that she had tried to commit suicide, which she refutes.

'I was so exhausted because of everything that all I wanted to do was sleep . . . and I did, right through to the following afternoon.' *Princess Margaret*

It was not until 1976 that stories of Margaret's relationship with Roddy hit the newspapers – when a photograph of them together in swimwear on Mustique was published. Tony himself was involved with Lucy Lindsay-Hogg, but their relationship did not reach the papers. On 19 March 1976 a joint statement was issued.

'Her Royal Highness The Princess Margaret, Countess of Snowdon, and the Earl of Snowdon have mutually agreed to live apart. The Princess will carry out her public duties and functions unaccompanied by Lord Snowdon. There are no plans for divorce proceedings.'

'The Queen is naturally very sad at what has happened. There has been no pressure from the Queen on either Princess Margaret or Lord Snowdon to take any particular course.' *Ronald Allison, the Queen's Press Secretary*

Tony was interviewed on television about the separation.

'I am naturally desperately sad in every way that this had to come. I would just like to say three things: firstly to pray for the understanding of our two children; secondly to wish Princess Margaret every happiness for her future; thirdly to express with the utmost humility my love, admiration and respect I will always have for her sister, her mother and indeed her entire family.' *Lord Snowdon*

Princess Margaret's appraisal of her husband's speech:
'The best act I've seen in years.'

'I cannot talk about my feelings for Princess Margaret or her feelings for me. That is a taboo subject.' *Roddy Llewellyn*

In 1978 Margaret was in hospital with hepatitis, and during this time her husband told her that he wanted a divorce. This statement was issued on 10 May:
'Her Royal Highness The Princess Margaret, Countess of Snowdon, and the Earl of Snowdon, after two years of separation have agreed that their marriage should formally be ended. Accordingly Her Royal Highness will start the necessary legal proceedings.'

To waiting reporters:
'I hope you will give support and encouragement to Princess Margaret when she comes out of hospital and goes about her duties again.' *Lord Snowdon*

The divorce was finalised on 11 July 1978. In September, still convalescing, Margaret went on a tour of the South Pacific, during which she became very ill again, this time with viral pneumonia.
'I very nearly died.' *Princess Margaret*

On 15 December 1978 Tony married Lucy Lindsay-Hogg, and their daughter, Lady Frances, was born seven months later on 17 July 1979. Roddy Llewellyn married Tatiana Soskin on 11 July 1981, and in April 1982 some newspapers carried reports that Margaret herself was going to marry her current escort, the businessman Norman Lonsdale, especially when it was noticed that she was wearing a ring on the third finger of her left hand.
'Absolute rubbish!' *Princess Margaret*

'I have never proposed marriage to Princess Margaret and I am not likely to do so in the foreseeable future. I

'When a 51-year-old woman, the mother of a twenty-year-old son, puts a 25-year-old ring on her finger, it does not mean she is going to get married.' *Princess Margaret*

have a great deal of respect for her. I think she has an extremely good brain, she knows a great deal about the theatre, ballet and that sort of thing. She is extremely stimulating to be with . . . a very outspoken person . . . what she has to say is usually right.' *Norman Lonsdale*

'Remarriage would be a devil of a trouble. And one would not want to be a bind. But if one did find someone nice . . .' *Princess Margaret*

'I have always regarded her as a bird in a gilded cage. She would have loved to break free, but was never able to.' *Jocelyn Stevens, close friend*

'I cannot imagine anything more wonderful than to be who I am.' *Princess Margaret*

THE REAL PRINCESS
MARGARET

'I'm no angel but I'm no Bo-Peep either.' *Princess Margaret*

'I have no ambition. Isn't that terrible?' *Princess Margaret*

About her often mentioned beautiful cornflower blue eyes:
'The only thing about me worth looking at.' *Princess Margaret*

About her 'acid-drop' or angry look:
'A defence mechanism. I'm not aware that I am doing it.' *Princess Margaret*

On her musical abilities:
'I once composed a lament, words as well as music. That was after Peter Townsend and I knew we couldn't get married.' *Princess Margaret*

'People don't like me when I get fat, but I seem to have been alternately fat or thin on a two years' basis.' *Princess Margaret*

Asked how she managed to lose weight:
'It's simple. I don't eat.' *Princess Margaret*

Asked whether any of her work is boring:
'No. Some of the things one does can be, but I've got a reflex against it now. I think it's very much up to one not to be bored.' *Princess Margaret*

'I leap at the opportunity of doing lots of different things to help my sister.' *Princess Margaret*

'I have as much privacy as a goldfish in a bowl.' *Princess Margaret*

'In our family, we do not have rifts. A very occasional row, but never a rift.' *Princess Margaret*

Of the new young Royal generation:
'When the young ones grow up, old Auntie won't be needed.' *Princess Margaret*

About her house, Les Jolies Eaux, on Mustique:
'Mustique is *my* country home.' *Princess Margaret*

'It is the only square inch of the world I own.' *Princess Margaret*

'I had always longed to build a house – with one's own ideas about cosy corners . . . It was great fun to do though difficult from a distance. I had to do it all from England . . . I put up a portrait of the Queen for people from abroad to see it's an English house.' *Princess Margaret*

On picnics:
'Nearly all picnics in the country end up, in desperation, in a lay-by because no one can decide where to stop. In my opinion, picnics should always be eaten at a table, sitting on a chair.' *Princess Margaret*

On the Beatles:
'I adored them because they were poets as well as musicians.' *Princess Margaret*

About entertaining with Lord Snowdon:
'We both hated black-tie and when we invited friends to dinner, the men always asked what they should wear. We said anything but black-tie, and they always came in the most beautiful shirts.' *Princess Margaret*

'I am convinced I look ridiculous in a hat.' *Princess Margaret*

'I never wore mini-skirts which were very high.' *Princess Margaret*

On seeing an old picture of herself in a mini:
'I can't believe I actually looked like that.' *Princess Margaret*

THE OUTSPOKEN PRINCESS

To a police committee chairman who asked her after a luncheon, 'How shall I introduce you – "Your Royal Highness" or what?'
'Does it really matter? You've been calling me "love" for the last two hours.' *Princess Margaret*

On hearing rumours that Princess Michael of Kent was moving to America:
'Yes, we thought we'd got rid of her.' *Princess Margaret*

On meeting Boy George:
'I don't know who he is, but he looks like an over made-up tart. I refuse to be photographed with him. I'm too old for that sort of thing.' *Princess Margaret*

Warning her sister about an approaching visit to Morocco:
'Going to Morocco, you'll find, is rather like being kidnapped; you never know where you are going or with whom.' *Princess Margaret*

THE REAL LORD SNOWDON

'I am not a member of the Royal Family, I am married to a member of the Royal Family.' *Lord Snowdon*

'Basically I am a carpenter.' *Lord Snowdon*

'His camera is so closely attached to him it's like an extra limb.' *Princess Margaret*

Why he gave up shooting:
'Any idiot can be a good shot; apart from that, I simply do not want to kill things any more.' *Lord Snowdon*

SNOWDON ON PHOTOGRAPHY

'It is an applied art, not one of the fine arts. I think a photographic print is only worth the paper it is printed on.' *Lord Snowdon*

'My aim is to move someone looking at my photography emotionally – either to happiness or sadness, but mainly to *think*.' *Lord Snowdon*

'If there is something I don't want in the picture, I will cut it out and alter the shape. If one's eye goes to something that is not necessary to the composition, I will paint it out. This is totally dishonest cheating, but I think the longer you photograph and the older you get, the simpler you want pictures to become.' *Lord Snowdon*

'There's always something wrong with one's photograph. If ever I took one I was pleased with, then I would stop. You always see something wrong – with the moment, the composition, the mood, the colour.' *Lord Snowdon*

'The only time you enjoy a picture is before you see it.' *Lord Snowdon*

About photographing children:
'You just have to sit around half the night waiting for a good expression. I know – I've had plenty of experience.' *Lord Snowdon*

Why she never offers anyone a light:
'Every time I lend my lighter, somebody pinches it.' *Princess Margaret*

'A photograph is *not* something to be framed and put on a wall.' *Lord Snowdon*

PRINCESS MARGARET — ON THE PRESS —

I have been misreported and misrepresented since the age of seventeen.' *Princess Margaret*

On her first remembered misinterpretation:
'I was with some of my fellow Sea Rangers in a boat on the lake at Frogmore. And *what* do you think appeared in the newspapers? They said I had pulled the bung from the bottom of the boat! That made me frightfully cross. I was part of a *team* and very proud of it, I might tell you. I would never have dreamt of doing something so irresponsible.' *Princess Margaret*

During a phase of popularity in 1973, Margaret looked back over the criticism of the past.
'I had no way to retaliate. I just had to submit and keep quiet. They accused me of everything, and I did not have the chance to give an interview to put the record straight. All that is different now. Apart from taking my clothes off and bathing in the fountains of Trafalgar Square, I can do anything.' *Princess Margaret*

Why she was always being attacked by the Beaverbrook newspapers:
'I was always told that it was because Lord Beaverbrook couldn't openly attack my father; my sister never did anything wrong – and anyway she married the right man – so he attacked me instead.' *Princess Margaret*

ON THEIR CHILDREN

'We don't want them to be treated in any extra special way. Where somebody works or is born is totally irrelevant. It's what people *do* with their lives.' *Lord Snowdon*

'They chose their own school, Bedales, themselves. All the people I've met from there come out with a kind of individuality and extremely free kind of mixed security and ambition that is good.' *Lord Snowdon*

To Lady Sarah:
'Remember you are a human being first and a Lady second.' *Lord Snowdon*

'We were taught to go on – with the flu, fever, whatever. One of the things I taught my children is, whenever you say you're going some place, never chuck it. And especially, never chuck one invitation for a better one.' *Princess Margaret*

'No one wants to date me because of who I am.' *Lady Sarah Armstrong-Jones*

LADY SARAH ARMSTRONG-JONES

'An oracle of youth at its most sensible.' *The Queen Mother*

'She's absolutely magic. It's impossible not to like her.' *Lord Lichfield*

'I'm very proud of her.' *Lord Snowdon*

'I don't think she has any ambitions to be a fashion leader.' *Lord Snowdon*

Furious at a girl who kept staring at Princess Margaret during a school function:
'She came here because she's my mother, not to be looked at. But of course she doesn't mind. Anyway, she's much better looking than *your* mother.' *Lady Sarah Armstrong-Jones*

'I like to give her freedom of choice and she is still finding out what she wants to do. If she wanted to be a train driver, that would be her decision.' *Lord Snowdon*

'Sarah is definitely a creative person but not a money-maker.' *Lord Snowdon*

VISCOUNT LINLEY

'A lot of rubbish is talked about my childhood. I had a totally normal upbringing, and not that different from anyone else.' *Viscount Linley*

'You don't spend much of your childhood at home, do you? One is away at school most of the time.' *Viscount Linley*

'I suppose the most important influence in my life has been my father.' *Viscount Linley*

'People come up and say, "You're so rich anyway". They imagine because Mummy's Mummy you come out with a wad of cash. I wish it were true.' *Viscount Linley*

About the school for craftsmen in wood: 'We have to work extremely hard here, but all the things we make are of exceptionally high quality.' *Viscount Linley*

Asked what was the first thing he had ever made:
'A mess.' *Viscount Linley*

Asked in 1983 what he would give his worst enemy:
'Dinner for two with Princess Michael of Kent.' *Viscount Linley*

Later asked to comment on that quip:
'I don't remember saying that! It's quite funny, isn't it? But I probably didn't say it at all.' *Viscount Linley*

The victim's reaction:
'Lord Linley has apologised to me, of course. We are now the greatest of friends. I shall look upon it all as a terrible misunderstanding.' *Princess Michael of Kent.*

'Most of my ancestors have been artistic.' *Viscount Linley*

'I don't know if the name will be an asset. It's certainly very hard to live up to.' *Viscount Linley*

On becoming a cabinet-maker in 1981:
'I didn't really choose my career. I just started it at school and liked it. I don't think that one ought to be doing this kind of work if money were the most important thing. I do it for the thrill of creating different things all the time.' *Viscount Linley*

About his father's work:
'He's the tops as far as I am concerned photographically – I could hardly say anything else, could I?' *Viscount Linley*

4

THE PRINCE
&
PRINCESS OF WALES

PRINCE CHARLES

Prince Charles was born on Sunday 14 November 1948, the first child of Princess Elizabeth and her husband the Duke of Edinburgh. His grandfather, George VI, was King, his mother was heir presumptive to the throne and would be Queen one day, and he in his turn would be King. But the children of Princesses do not automatically become Princes themselves – and his father had not yet been made a Prince of the United Kingdom. It looked as if the future King would be known simply as plain Charles Mountbatten. So shortly before Charles's birth, George VI had to issue a royal order to the effect that all Elizabeth's children could have the title Prince or Princess and be called Royal Highness.

Announcement: 'Her Royal Highness the Princess Elizabeth, Duchess of Edinburgh, was safely delivered of a Prince at 9.14 o'clock this evening. Her Royal Highness and the infant Prince are both doing well.'

Telling the young Prince Charles how to perform the Royal wave:
'This is how you do it. It is like opening a huge jar of sweets.' *The Queen Mother*

'The Queen says that she thinks the baby is like his mother, but the Duke is quite certain that the baby is very like himself.' *Countess Granville (aunt)*

What the baby reminded his father of:
'A plum pudding.' *Prince Philip*

'He has an interesting pair of hands for a baby. They are rather large, but fine with long fingers – quite unlike mine and certainly unlike his father's. It will be interesting to see what they will become.' *Princess Elizabeth*

The new mother received 4000 telegrams of congratulations on the night of his birth, and a huge crowd partied outside Buckingham Palace well into the night:
'It's wonderful to think, isn't it, that his arrival could give a bit of happiness to so many people, besides ourselves, at this time?' *Princess Elizabeth*

'I suppose I'll now be known as Charley's Aunt.' *Princess Margaret*

On 6 February 1952 King George VI died. Charles found the Queen Mother in tears.
'Don't cry, granny.' *Prince Charles*

'I've learnt the way a monkey learns – by watching its parents.' *Prince Charles*

Prince Charles, almost four, passing a courtier in the corridor:
Prince Charles: 'What are you doing here?'
Courtier: 'I'm going to see the Queen.'
Prince Charles: 'Who's she?'

On learning that he was to be King one day:
'I didn't suddenly wake up in my pram one day and say "Yippee" . . . It just dawns on you slowly that people are interested . . . and slowly you get the idea that you have a certain duty and responsibility. It's better that way, rather than someone suddenly telling you "You must do this" and "You must do that", because of who you are.
It's one of those things you grow up in.' *Prince Charles*

The Queen had to go on a royal tour shortly after Charles's fourth birthday. He followed her progress on a globe.
'Mummy has an important job to do. [pointing to Australia] She's down there.' *Prince Charles*

The young Prince Charles and Princess Anne hearing a military band outside Buckingham Palace:
Anne: 'Is it another Coronation?'
Prince Charles: 'Don't be silly. The next Coronation will be mine.'

'Mummy, what *are* schoolboys?' *Prince Charles*

'The Queen and I want Charles to go to school with other boys of his generation and learn to live with other children, and to absorb from childhood the discipline imposed by education with others.' *Prince Philip*

In January 1957 Prince Charles started as a day boy at Hill House school.
'Look, I'm only going to bother if you're permanently bottom. I really couldn't care less where you are. Just stay in the middle, that's all I ask.' *Prince Philip*

In September 1957 Charles became a boarder at Cheam school in Surrey.
'You won't be able to jump up and down on *these* beds.' *The Queen*

'He felt family separation very deeply. He dreaded going away to school.' *Mabel Anderson (nanny)*

'It is the wishes of the Queen and Prince Philip that there shall be no alteration in the way the school is run and that Prince Charles shall be treated the same as the other boys . . . His parents' wishes are that he should be given exactly the same education and upbringing as the other boys at the school.' *The headmaster of Cheam*

Writing his first letter home from Cheam:
'I know my mother is Queen, but how do I put that on the envelope?' *Prince Charles*

On being told that if he didn't hurry up with his chores he would get into trouble:
'I can't help that. I must do my duties.' *Prince Charles*

On playing rugger at Cheam:
'They always put me in the second row, the worst place in the scrum.' *Prince Charles*

On the standard school prayer for the Royal Family, including himself:
'I wish they prayed for the other boys too.' *Prince Charles*

On 26 July 1958 the Queen broadcast a message at the Commonwealth Games in Cardiff.
'I intend to create my son Charles Prince of Wales today. When he is grown up I will present him to you at Caernarvon.'

On hearing the announcement over the radio at school:
'I remember being acutely embarrassed when it was announced. I heard this marvellous great cheer coming from the stadium in Cardiff, and I think for a little boy of nine it was rather bewildering. All the others turned and looked at me in amazement.' *Prince Charles*

Gordonstoun was the tough school in Scotland at which his father had been a pupil. Charles started there in May 1962.
'How can you treat a boy as just an ordinary chap when his mother's portrait is on the coins you spend in the school shop, on the stamps you put on your letters home, and when a detective follows him wherever he goes? Most boys tend to fight shy of friendship with Charles. The result is he is very lonely. It is this loneliness, rather than the school's toughness, which must be hardest on him.' *A boy who was at Gordonstoun at the same time as Charles*

His grandmother worried about him at Gordonstoun.
'He is a very gentle boy, with a very kind heart, which I think is the essence of everything.' *The Queen Mother*

In July 1963 Charles was in an hotel on the Isle of Lewis with a school party when a crowd gathered to gawp at him. Not knowing how to cope, he ducked into the bar and bought himself a cherry brandy. A reporter happened to be there, and the 'scandal' of his under-age drinking became news around the world.

'I thought "I can't bear this anymore" and went off somewhere else. The only other place was the bar. Having never been into a bar before, the first thing I thought of doing was having a drink, of course. And being terrified, not knowing what to do, I said the first drink that came into my head, which happened to be cherry brandy, because I'd drunk it before when it was cold out shooting. Hardly had I taken a sip when the whole world exploded round my ears.' *Prince Charles*

In 1966 Charles spent seven months at a school in Australia. Timbertop was the country outpost of Geelong school 'the Eton of Australia'. As an older pupil he was also in charge of groups of younger boys.

On life at Timbertop:
'Almost everyone, masters and boys, enjoy themselves up here. One never seems to stop running here and there for one minute of the day . . . You virtually have to inspect every inch of the ground you hope to put your tent on in case there are any ants or other ghastly creatures. There is one species of ant called Bull Ants which are three-quarters of an inch long, and they bite like mad . . . At the camp site the cooking is done on an open fire in a trench. You have to be very careful in hot weather that you don't start a bush fire, and at the beginning of this term there was a total ban in force, so that you ate all the tinned food cold.' *Prince Charles*

On the improvement in Charles after his time in Australia:
'I went out there with a boy, and returned with a man.' *Prince Charles's private detective*

Of his time in Australia:
'I absolutely adored it.' *Prince Charles*

In a letter home from Timbertop:
'The first week I was here, I was made to go out and chop logs on a hillside in boiling hot weather. I could hardly see my hands for blisters.' *Prince Charles*

On his first attempt at sheep-shearing:
'I made rather a mess of it, and left a somewhat shredded sheep.' *Prince Charles*

'Australia got me over my shyness.' *Prince Charles*

During the school holiday Charles went to Papua New Guinea.

'We arrived at the entrance to the village and the drums stopped and the whole village was assembled there and for some unknown reason they suddenly started to sing "God Save the Queen", and it was the most moving, touching thing I have ever experienced, I think, to see these people, miles from Britain, singing the National Anthem. And the tears practically rolled down my cheeks.' *Prince Charles*

'In Australia you are judged on how people see you and feel about you. There are no assumptions. You have to fend for yourself.' *Prince Charles*

'The most wonderful experience I've ever had.' *Prince Charles*

Looking back at his time at Gordonstoun:
'I did not enjoy school as much as I might have, but this was because I am happier at home than anywhere else . . . I had this schoolboy dream that I was going to escape and hide in the forest, in a place where no one could find me, so that I wouldn't have to go back to school. I hated that institution, just as I hated leaving home. When you lead a perfectly agreeable existence you don't want to go back to cold showers at seven in the morning and a quick run before breakfast . . . But Gordonstoun developed my will-power and self-control, helped me to discipline myself, and I think that discipline, not in the sense of making you bath in cold water, but in the Latin sense – giving shape and form and tidiness to your life – is the most important thing your education can do.' *Prince Charles*

After Geelong, Charles went back to Gordonstoun to take his 'A' levels. He was also elected 'Guardian' or head boy. Around this time he took up the cello, having found he had no talent for the trumpet.

'There was a wonderful German lady who had been there for years; she was there when my father was there. She kept turning round in the middle of the orchestra and saying: "Ach ze trumpet, I cannot stand ze trumpet." So I decided to give it up.' *Prince Charles*

After Gordonstoun top-level discussions about what Charles should do next were held. One conference included the Archbishop of Canterbury, Harold Wilson (the then Prime Minister) and Earl Mountbatten among other equally illustrious men. Mountbatten was the one to state the formula which came to be followed almost exactly:
'Trinity College like his grandfather; Dartmouth like his father and grandfather; and then to sea in the Royal Navy, ending up with a command of his own.' Earl Mountbatten

Charles started at Trinity College Cambridge in 1966.
A huge crowd greeted his arrival:
Voice in crowd: 'Good luck!'
Charles: 'Thanks! I'll need it!'

The day of arrival:
'All I could see were serried ranks of variously trousered legs from which I had to distinguish those of the Master and the Senior Tutor... My most vivid memory of that day is of several burly, bowler-hatted gentlemen (the College Porters) dragging shut those magnificent wooden gates to prevent the crowd from following in. It was like a scene from the French Revolution.' Prince Charles

On going to university:
'Marvellous to have three years when you are not bound by anything, and not married, and haven't got any particular job.' Prince Charles

Fellow students avoided Charles for fear that they would be considered toadies. He did, however, make friends with a young socialist, and fired by their talks had a question to put to his Master, R A Butler:
Prince Charles: 'Do you think it would be all right if I joined the University Labour Club?'
Butler 'Hell, no!'

Charles attended a student demonstration in disguise.

'I wanted to see what they were like. I do try and understand what they are getting at, but I can't help feeling that a lot of it is purely for the sake of change, and for the sake of doing something to change things – which, from my point of view, is pointless.' *Prince Charles*

Regretting Trinity's relaxation of its 'gate laws':

'It was a great challenge to climb over the wall. Half the fun of university life is breaking the rules.' *Prince Charles*

Impressions of Trinity, in Varsity, *the university magazine*:

'Every modulation of light and weather, like the orange-pink glow from the stone of the Wren Library in the last rays from a wintry sun . . . the everlasting splashing of the Great Court fountain . . . and the everlasting sound of photographers' boots ringing on the cobbles . . . the grinding note of an Urban District Council dust lorry's engine rising and falling in spasmodic energy at seven o'clock in the morning, accompanied by the monotonous jovial dustman's refrain of "O Come all Ye Faithful" and the headsplitting clang of the dustbins.' *Prince Charles* (*After this was published the rubbish collection was put back to a later hour, and the dustman was invited to make a record.*)

Charles got a good grade in his first year exams in Archaeology and Anthropology, and Butler thought he stood 'a damn good chance of a First' in the subjects. But Charles decided to switch and study the British Constitution.
Butler: 'Why?'
Prince Charles: 'Because I'm probably going to be King.'

On an official tour of a power station during one vacation he met a fellow student, who said he was doing a vacation job.
'That makes two of us.' *Prince Charles*

In preparation for his Investiture as Prince of Wales at Caernarvon, Charles went to Aberystwyth University for a term to study Welsh. The Investiture, and his going to Aberystwyth, was very unpopular with the Welsh.

Of his time at Aberystwyth:
'I haven't many friends, there haven't been many parties.' *Prince Charles*

Seeing a group of demonstrators while meeting George Thomas, the then Welsh Secretary of State:
Prince Charles: 'I'm going to talk to them.'
George Thomas: 'I would advise against it, sir.'
Prince Charles: 'I know you would, but I'm going.'

Charles tried to talk to the demonstrators.
'I asked this chap who was holding a banner what it meant. He just hurled abuse at me. So after I'd asked more questions I gave up. There was no point.' *Prince Charles*

About the Welsh demonstrating against the Investiture:
'I don't blame people demonstrating like that. They've never seen me before. They don't know what I'm like. I've hardly been to Wales, and you can't expect people to be over-zealous about the fact of having a so-called English Prince amongst them and be frightfully excited about it.' *Prince Charles*

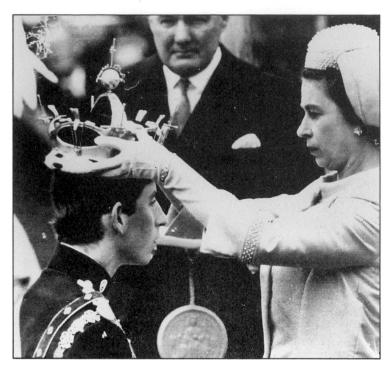

'When he stood up and started to speak in Welsh, he wasn't just a boy. He was a Prince. You could have put a suit of armour on that lad and sent him off to Agincourt.' *The Mayor of Caernarvon*

'He came, saw and conquered the Welsh.' *Prince Philip*

'If I've learnt anything in the last eight weeks, it's been about Wales in particular and its problems, and what these people feel about Wales. They're depressed about what might happen if they don't try and preserve the language and culture, which is unique and special to Wales. And if something is unique and special, I think it's well worth preserving.' *Prince Charles*

Was he nervous about the Investiture?
'It would be unnatural if one didn't feel any apprehension. One always wonders what's going to happen in this sort of thing. But I think if one takes it as it comes, it'll be much easier . . . As long as I don't get covered too much in egg and tomato, I'll be all right.' *Prince Charles*

On the cost of the Investiture:
'Spending £200,000 or £250,000 or whatever it is on an apparently useless ceremony . . . does not get you positively anywhere, unless you think: "Oh well, we shall get some return in tourism, or investment from interested Americans." My view of the situation is that if you are going to have a ceremony like this you should spend enough money to make it dignified, colourful and worthy of Britain. But you should not spend too much.' *Prince Charles*

From a speech he made in Welsh, three weeks before the Investiture:
'I have found time to read Dafydd ap Gwilym [a Welsh poet] in bed – and now I know something of the girls of Llanbadarn.' *Prince Charles*

When he turned on the television to see himself, yet again, in the pre-Investiture run-up:
'It's always me. I'm getting rather sick of my face.' *Prince Charles*

Looking back at the Investiture years later: 'Welsh nationalism was as its height. Some of it was directed against me, understandably. It was embarrassing, but I could understand the problem. I believe that when I went to spend some time in Wales and showed my interest and concern about Welsh affairs (and tried to learn the language) a bit of the hot air may have gone out of the more negative forms of Welsh Nationalism. I hope that doesn't sound pompous or conceited; I like to think it's true.' *Prince Charles*

After the Investiture, Charles went back to university to take his finals, which he passed with an average 2, II grade. He also gained his grade A private pilot's licence. In March 1971 he joined the RAF as Flight Lieutenant and in September he joined the Royal Navy as Acting Sub-Lieutenant.

'It is pointless and ill-informed to say that I am entering a profession trained in killing. The Services in the first place are there for fast, efficient and well-trained action in defence. Surely the Services must attract a large number of duty-conscious people? Otherwise who else would subject themselves to being square-bashed, shouted at by petty officers and made to do ghastly things in Force Ten gales? I am entering the RAF and then the Navy because I believe I can contribute something to this country by so doing. To me it is a worthwhile occupation, and one which I am convinced will stand me in good stead for the rest of my life.' *Prince Charles*

In July 1971 he took his first parachute jump – which nearly went disastrously wrong as his feet caught in the rigging.

'It was very odd. Either I've got hollow legs or something. It doesn't often happen. The first thing I thought was "They didn't tell me anything about this." Fortunately, my feet weren't twisted around the lines, and they came out very quickly. The Royal Marines were roaring around in little rubber boats underneath, and I was out of the water within ten seconds . . . A rather hairy experience.' *Prince Charles*

Charles, scruffy and unshaven was leaning over the side of his ship when some photographers ask him where they could find the Prince.
'Prince Charles? Oh, he won't see you. He's a pretty nasty piece of work you know.' *Prince Charles*

When fellow officers attempted to de-bag him:
'I can send you to the Tower you know. It's quite within my power.' *Prince Charles*

In February 1976 Charles was made captain of the minehunter HMS Bronington, *and he left the Services that December having been promoted to Wing Commander in the RAF and Commander in the Royal Navy.*

Of his time in the Navy:
'It's given me a marvellous opportunity to get as close to the "ordinary" British chap as possible.' *Prince Charles*

'I can hardly believe I don't have to go back to sea immediately . . . I used to have a terrible time filled with horror and wondering what would happen . . . I always used to get very nervous – especially when I had to bring the ship alongside. My knees knocked together so violently I had to tie pieces of sorbo rubber between them to stop them demoralising the troops.' *Prince Charles*

In the 1980s Charles became increasingly concerned about deprivation in inner city areas, devoting much attention to both the environment and the quality of life of young people. In 1983, during a visit to Manchester community centre, he was asked if he minded being the target for a custard pie:
'Don't ask me. Just do it.' *Prince Charles*

Looking back years later:
'I could have stayed in the Navy, I suppose. I could have concentrated purely on being a Naval Officer. But there were difficulties with that because I would only have stayed if I could have gone on flying, which was my main love in the Navy. And it was becoming more and more difficult, because people get into a terrible state about me flying you know – if I am going to fly myself into a hill, sea or whatever.' *Prince Charles*

On his envy of Prince Andrew's hands-on military experience in the Falklands War:
'I never had that chance to test myself. It's terribly important to see how you react, to be tested.' *Prince Charles*

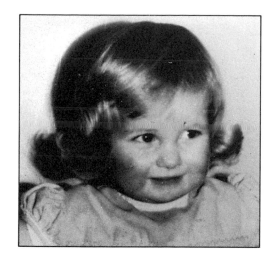

'She was a delightful child, and as a baby she could have won any beauty competition.' *Earl Spencer*

THE PRINCESS OF WALES

Diana Frances Spencer was born on 1 July 1961 at Park House Sandringham, the third daughter of Frances and Edward 'Johnny' Althorp. Her father was a former equerry to the Queen, and her mother was the daughter of Ruth, Lady Fermoy, lady-in-waiting to The Queen Mother. Diana did not become Lady Diana Spencer until 1975 when her father became Earl Spencer.

'She loved her soft toys nearly as much as she loved babies. She always loved babies.' *Earl Spencer*

'Duchess.' *The Spencer family nickname for Diana*

Diana's parents separated when she was six. 'I'll never marry unless I really love someone. If you're not really sure you love someone, then you might get divorced. I never want to be divorced!' *Diana Spencer*

When she was nine Diana was sent away to board at Riddlesworth Hall school in Norfolk.
'She was awfully sweet with the little ones.' *The headmistress*

Diana started a new school, West Heath in Kent, when she was 12. Although she wasn't academic, Diana was good at dancing and sport.

'When she dived you never heard a splash.' *The headmistress*

'She's a girl who notices what needs to be done, then does it willingly and cheerfully. The dining room staff liked her a lot because she used to help them with laying the tables and clearing up.' *The headmistress*

Opening a new sports hall at the school years later when a Princess:

'Perhaps now, when future generations are handed out punishments for talking after lights, pillow fights, illegal food, they will be told to run six times round this hall. It has to be preferable to the lacrosse pitch or weeding the garden, which I became a great expert at.' *The Princess of Wales*

'We used to be very naughty sliding down the back of the bath.' *The Princess of Wales*

'My years at West Heath were certainly very happy ones. I made many friends whom I often see and in spite of what Miss Rudge and my other teachers may have thought, I did actually learn something, though you would not have known by my 'O' level results.' *The Princess of Wales*

In 1976 Earl Spencer married his second wife, Raine, the daughter of Barbara Cartland, initially not a popular choice with the Spencer children.

'They won't accept me. Whatever I do is wrong. I just want us to be one close family.' *Countess Spencer to Barbara Cartland*

'I never got any 'O' levels – always too busy. Brain the size of a pea, I've got.' *The Princess of Wales*

'I actually wanted to be a dancer, but overshot the height by a long way.' *Lady Diana*

Remembering her early childhood:
'A good time of my life.' *Diana Spencer*

When she was sixteen in 1978, Diana attended a finishing school in Switzerland, called Institut Alpin Videmanette.

'While Diana was a pretty girl she was not the beauty she's blossomed into now. She knew she wanted to work with children, to get married and have a family of her own, and she once told me that she would only marry for love not for money or position.' *Diana's French teacher*

At school Diana had kept a photograph of Prince Charles above her bed. She was never remotely interested in other men.

'Chaps would meet Diana and fall instantly in love. Many tried to win her, sending flowers and begging for a date, but she always politely declined.' *Simon Berry, a friend of Diana's*

'Lady Diana, I can assure you, has never had a lover. There is no such thing as her ever having had a past.' *Lord Fermoy (uncle)*

'I'm a normal person, hopefully, who loves life.' *Lady Diana*

'I'm a perfectionist with myself though not necessarily with everyone else.' *Lady Diana*

THE ROMANCE

Charles and Diana met for the first time in 1977 when Diana was sixteen.

'Prince Charles came to stay as a friend in my sister's house for a shoot, and we sort of met in a ploughed field.' *Lady Diana*

Charles's first impressions of Diana:

'I remember thinking what a very jolly and amusing and attractive sixteen-year-old she was. Great fun – bouncy and full of life.' *Prince Charles*

Diana's first impressions of Charles:

'Pretty amazing.' *Lady Diana*

But the romance really started in the summer of 1980, when Diana was invited to join the Royal Family for a short stay.

'They both have the same sense of humour – she's giggly and so is he. He loved ballet, opera and sport, and so does she. He met Miss Right and she met Mr Right. They just clicked.' *Lady Sarah Spencer*

The press soon got wind of this new girl in Charles's life, and in September 1980 began to lay siege to 'Lady Di' as she was dubbed. Slowly bits about her life began to be revealed in the papers.

'I shudder when I hear her called Lady Di. No one in her life has ever called her Di.' *The Honourable Mrs Frances Shand Kydd*

'I go everywhere I can by bike.' *Lady Diana*

'I haven't got a background . . . That's what everybody else seems to have. I mean I haven't had a *chance* to have a background like that. I'm only nineteen.' *Lady Diana*

'I share my flat with three other girls – who pay me rent for living here. Until this publicity started, we led perfectly ordinary lives. Now everyone seems to know who I am. I'm not worried about it – but I'm certainly not used to it.' *Lady Diana*

'I'm an avid reader. I'll read almost anything I can get my hands on – from women's magazines to Charles Dickens. Don't make me sound like a bookworm – because I'm not. I read because I enjoy it and I find it relaxing. Especially when I think of the photographers waiting outside to chase me round the block.' *Lady Diana*

'Anyone in my situation would be feeling the pressure. However I'm still bearing up, in spite of all the attention surrounding me. I haven't been carted off yet. I'm still around. I'm getting to know the reporters. I feel sorry for them having to wait outside my flat in all weathers.' *Lady Diana*

On Charles:
'You know I cannot say anything about the Prince or my feelings for him. I am saying that off my own bat. No one has told me to keep quiet. I'm sorry. It must be a real bore for you.' *Lady Diana*

On why she wouldn't say more:
'You see, my sister Sarah was going out with Charles last year. She talked to the press too much I think and they *murdered* her.' *Lady Diana*

'Many articles have been labelled "exclusive quotes", when the plain truth is that my daughter has not spoken the words attributed to her. Fanciful speculation, if it is in good taste, is one thing, but this can be embarrassing. Lies are quite another matter, and by their nature hurtful and inexcusable . . . May I ask the editors of Fleet Street whether, in the execution of their jobs, they consider it necessary or fair to harass my daughter daily, from dawn until well after dusk? Is it fair to ask any human

'The whole thing's got out of control. I'm not so much bored as miserable. Everywhere I go there's someone there . . . If I go to a restaurant or just out shopping to the supermarket, they're trying to take photographs . . . It makes everyone else's life so bloody, particularly the girls who share my flat . . . It's a situation I think the Royal Family is not really aware of. I don't think they really know what's going on down here . . . You see, they've all grown up with it, so they know what to do because they're used to it.' *Lady Diana*

being, regardless of circumstances, to be treated in this way?' *The Honourable Mrs Frances Shand Kydd*

The press tried to draw her family into talking about the romance.
'I have three daughters and the Queen has three unmarried sons. They have all been invited to stay at Balmoral and Sandringham. Diana was recently invited back for the fourth time – so she obviously hasn't blotted her copybook . . . I don't think her friendship with Prince Charles is any more than that. I think people are reading too much into it.' *Earl Spencer*

But throughout all this, the romance was blossoming.
'I began to realise what was going on in my mind, and hers in particular.' *Prince Charles*

'Even *I* don't know what's going on.' *The Queen*

'The idea of this romance going on for another year is intolerable.' *The Queen*

On Diana being harassed by photographers:
'Well she's going to have to learn to get used to this sort of thing. At least it's useful in that respect.' *The Queen*

'She's a delightful girl. Charles could not find a more perfect partner.' *The Queen*

In September 1980 photographers took pictures of Diana with her young charges in the park. The light was behind her and her legs showed clearly through her skirt.
Charles's reaction:
'I knew your legs were good. But I didn't realise they were that spectacular. And did you really have to show them to everybody?' *Prince Charles*

Diana's reaction:
'I was so nervous about the whole thing I never thought I'd be standing with the light behind me. I don't want to be remembered for not having worn a petticoat.' *Lady Diana*

'I ended up in the papers with legs looking like a Steinway piano's!' *Lady Diana*

Prince Charles was asked about the romance while TV camera lights blinded him.
'I can't think what useful information to impart on an occasion like this, but judging by the brightness of the lights somebody must think I have something to say.' *Prince Charles*

'If you didn't laugh at some of these [stories in the press] you would go mad.' *Prince Charles*

In November 1980 Charles went on a tour of India, and the press asked Diana if she would miss him:
'I'm not going to say anything. Would you in my situation? I'm not planning to go out this evening. I intend watching *Dallas* on television.' *Lady Diana*

THE ENGAGEMENT

'When you marry in my position, you're going to marry someone who, perhaps, is one day going to be Queen. You've got to choose somebody very carefully, I think, who could fulfil this particular role, and it has got to be somebody pretty unusual.' *Prince Charles*

Charles proposed to Diana in February 1981 before she was to visit her mother in Australia for a holiday.

'I wanted to give Diana a chance to think about it – to think if it all was going to be too awful. She'd planned to go to Australia with her mother quite a long time before anyway, and I thought, "Well, I'll ask her then so that she'll have a chance of thinking it over while she's away, so she can decide if she can bear the whole idea – or not, as the case may be." ' *Prince Charles*

'I'm very conscious of the duties to come in the years ahead. I know I shall be happy. Charles will be there.' *Lady Diana*

When Diana confided to her father that she wanted to marry Charles:

Earl Spencer: 'You must only marry the man you love.'

Lady Diana: 'That is what I am doing.'

'Can I marry your daughter? I have asked her and very surprisingly she has said yes.' *Prince Charles to Earl Spencer*

'I wonder what he would have done if I'd refused!' *Earl Spencer*

'I saw Diana in her London flat and guessed when I saw her face. She was totally radiant, bouncing, bubbling, and I said: "You're engaged", and she said: "Yes".' *Lady Sarah Spencer*

Announcement made on 24 February 1981:
'It is with the greatest pleasure that the Queen and the Duke of Edinburgh announce the betrothal of their beloved son, the Prince of Wales, to the Lady Diana Spencer, daughter of the Earl of Spencer and the Honourable Mrs Shand Kydd.'

The proposal:
'If I were to ask, what do you think you might answer?' *Prince Charles*

'It wasn't a difficult decision. It was what I wanted – it is what I want.' *Lady Diana*

What they have in common:
'Sense of humour – every outdoor activity. Except I don't ride.' *Lady Diana*

'Skiing. She's a great skier, although I haven't seen her skiing yet.' *Prince Charles*

After the engagement:
'Sometimes I feel very worried, as if I'll never see her again – later, yes, but not for the first few years, when I'll be watching her, like everyone else, on telly.' *Earl Spencer*

While the press loved Earl Spencer, they were not so keen on his second wife.
'I'm absolutely sick of the Wicked Stepmother lark. You're never going to make me sound like a human being, because people like to think I'm Dracula's mother.' *Countess Spencer*

Diana moved into Clarence House to stay with the Queen Mother. She was sorry to leave her flatmates.
'For God's sake ring me up. I'm going to need you!' *Lady Diana*

About the ring:
'I can't get used to wearing it yet. The other day I even scratched my nose with it because it's so big – the ring I mean.' *Lady Diana*

On the age-gap between them:
'It's only twelve years. Lots of people have got married with that sort of age difference. I just feel you're only as old as you think you are . . . Diana will certainly keep me young . . . I think I shall be exhausted!' *Prince Charles*

'A hell of a lot of people I photograph do need more retouching than you can believe. Lady Diana does not happen to be one. She is very beautiful. There was no retouching done by me whatsoever. Lady Diana does not need retouching.' *Lord Snowdon*

Before the wedding Diana was one of the hosts at a Royal Garden Party at Buckingham Palace, where it rained hard.
'I shall sit down and sulk if it's like

this in Gibraltar [where they were to spend part of their honeymoon]. There'll be no rain left at this rate.' *Lady Diana*

To a blind lady at the same garden party: 'Do you want to feel my engagement ring? I'd better not lose it before Wednesday, or they won't know who I am.' *Lady Diana*

At the same party: 'We had a wedding rehearsal yesterday. Everybody was fighting. I got my heel stuck in some grating and everyone was saying "Hurry up, Diana." I said, "I can't. I'm stuck." ' *Lady Diana*

About the coming wedding: 'I'm going to videotape it. Then I'll be able to run back over the best bits – and when it comes to the part that says "I will", I'm going to take that out and put something else.' *Lady Diana*

About the wedding: 'I can't wait for the whole thing. I want everybody to come out, you know, having had a marvellous musical and emotional experience.' *Prince Charles*

The night before the wedding an interview with the couple was broadcast on BBC TV.
Lady Diana: 'We're not allowed to see each other the night before – we might quarrel.'
Interviewer: 'Has Prince Charles been a great help in recent months?'
Lady Diana: 'Marvellous! Oh, a tower of strength.'
Prince Charles: 'Gracious!'
Lady Diana: 'I had to say that because you're sitting there.'

On her future job:
'30 per cent fantastic, 70 per cent sheer slog.' *Lady Diana*

'I am absolutely delighted, thrilled, blissfully happy. I never had any doubts.' *Lady Diana*

THE WEDDING

The wedding took place on 29 July 1981 at St Paul's Cathedral.

On why they chose St Paul's rather than the more traditional Westminster Abbey:
'It is big enough to take one orchestra, if not two' *Prince Charles*

Before the wedding:
'I've just had an enormous breakfast. I hope that stops my tummy rumbling in St Paul's.' *Lady Diana*

'It's taken a bit of getting used to the camera. But it's wonderful to see people's enthusiastic reactions, a mass of smiling faces. It's most rewarding and gives me a tremendous boost.' *Lady Diana*

On first seeing his bride in her wedding dress:
Prince Charles: 'You look beautiful!'
Lady Diana: 'Beautiful for you.'

During the ceremony Diana repeated the names of her husband-to-be in the wrong order.
Lady Diana: 'Philip Charles Arthur George.'
Prince Andrew: 'She's married my father!'

When Charles was told that because of the longer distance between St Pauls and Buckingham Palace, the cost of soldiers to line the route would be enormous, his caustic reply was:
'Well stand them further apart.' *Prince Charles*

Prince Charles also muddled his vows and left out the word 'worldly' and promised to share all Diana's goods with her.
'*That* was no mistake!' *Princess Anne*

At the dance that evening:
'I'd love to stay and dance all night.' *The Queen*

On the balcony after the wedding breakfast the Prince and his new Princess delighted crowds with a public kiss.
The Princess of Wales: 'They want us to kiss!'
Prince Charles: 'Why not?'

THE HONEYMOON AND EARLY DAYS

'We still cannot get over what happened that day. Neither of us can get over the atmosphere; it was electric, I felt, and so did my wife. I remember several occasions that were similar, with large crowds: the Coronation and the Jubilee, and various major national occasions. All of them were very special in their own way but our wedding was quite extraordinary as far as we were concerned. It made us extraordinarily proud to be British.' *Prince Charles*

On married life:
'I can highly recommend it. It is a marvellous life.' *The Princess of Wales*

On looking at videocassettes of their wedding during their honeymoon:
'It's so wonderful to be able to catch up with all the things we missed.' *Prince Charles*

'I have the best mother-in-law in the world.' *The Princess of Wales*

For a while Diana completely eclipsed Charles in popularity, and wherever they went people wanted to see her rather than him.
'I'm going to have to get used to looking at the backs of photographers.' *Prince Charles*

'I'm just a collector of flowers these days. I haven't enough wives to go round.' *Prince Charles*

'I'm sorry, I've only got one wife and she's over there on the other side of the street. You'll have to make do with me instead.' *Prince Charles*

'She's not here, there's only me, so you'd better go and ask for your money back.' *Prince Charles*

CHARLES AND DIANA
AS PARENTS

Before marriage:
'I want lots and lots of children – at least as many as Queen Victoria.' *Lady Diana*

On 5 November 1981 it was announced that Diana was expecting her first child.
'Diana wants this baby very much. She will make a wonderful mother.' *Earl Spencer*

'Naturally I am absolutely delighted. It is wonderful and of course I feel like any prospective father. My wife is overjoyed as well. A baby will be marvellous.' *Prince Charles*

Diana suffered from morning sickness.
'She's finding pregnancy harder work than she expected.' *Prince Charles*

When Diana could not accompany Charles to an official occasion:
'She is quite all right, but it is better for her not to do too many things at present. You've all got wives – you know the problem.' *Prince Charles*

Asked if she wanted a boy or a girl:
'I don't mind, as long as it's healthy.' *The Princess of Wales*

Asked the same question nearer the birth:
'A boy, I hope, but we'll have to wait and see.' *The Princess of Wales*

Prince William was born on 21 June 1982 at 9.03 pm at St Mary's Hospital Paddington. His father was present at the birth.
'It was rather a grown-up thing. I found it rather a shock to my system.' *Prince Charles*

'No one told me it would be like this.'
The Princess of Wales

Charles's reaction immediately after the birth:
'relieved ... delighted ... overwhelmed ... over the moon.' *Prince Charles*

What did the baby look like?
'He looks marvellous. Fair, sort of blondish. He's not bad.' *Prince Charles*
Outside the hospital:
Voice in crowd: 'Nice one, Charlie. Let's have another one!'
Prince Charles: 'Bloody hell! Give us a chance. Ask my wife. I don't think she'd be too pleased yet.'

'The birth of our son has given us both more pleasure than you can imagine. It has made me incredibly proud and somewhat amazed.' *Prince Charles*

William Arthur Philip Louis cried all the way through his christening until Diana put her little finger in his mouth for him to suck.
'He's a good speech-maker.' *The Queen*

'My husband knows so much about rearing children that I've suggested he has the next one and I'll sit back and give advice.' *The Princess of Wales*

On their choice of Sir Laurens Van der Post as one of William's godparents:
'One of the reasons I asked Sir Laurens Van der Post to be a godfather was because he is one of the best story-tellers I have ever come across and I want my son to be able to sit on his godfather's knee and listen to his wonderful stories.' *Prince Charles*

On what she would most like for her 22nd birthday, during a trip to Canada:
'My perfect birthday present is going home. I can't wait to see William.' *The Princess of Wales*

On Charles as a father:
'He is a doting daddy and does everything perfectly.' *The Princess of Wales*

Diana insisting that it should be herself rather than the nanny that the children turned to.
'A mother's arms are so much more comforting.' *The Princess of Wales*

'I would like to bring up our children to be well-mannered, to think of other people, to put themselves in other people's positions, to do unto others as they would have done unto them. At the end of it, even if they are not very bright or very qualified, at least if they have reasonable manners they will get much further in life than by not having them.' *Prince Charles*

On 14 February 1984 it was announced that Diana was expecting a second child.

Two days later Charles visited a car factory.
Prince Charles: 'Your production here is going well.'
One of the workers: 'Your own production line is going well too.'

'I don't think I'm made for the production line. I haven't felt well since day one.' *The Princess of Wales*

'If men had to have babies they would only have one each.' *The Princess of Wales*

On 15 September at 4.20 pm Prince Henry Charles Albert David was born, later to be known as Harry.

On bringing up children:
'It's all hard work and no pay.' *The Princess of Wales*

Asked about William when he was a few months old:
Prince Charles: 'He's not at all shy. He's a great grinner, but he does dribble a lot.'
The Princess of Wales: 'He's just like his father.'

Showing the six-month-old Prince William off:
'I'm sorry he's not all that smiley today. They never do when you want them to. We'll probably get all those child specialists saying we handled him wrong.' *Prince Charles*

'It isn't only a woman's job to bring children up, of course. It's a man's job as well.' *Prince Charles*

To a soldier of the Welsh Guards:
Prince Charles: 'Any children yet?'
Soldier: 'Not yet; we are keeping our fingers crossed, sir.'
Prince Charles: 'You certainly won't get one that way!'

Visiting a Dr Barnardo's Home:
'I just can't understand how anybody can abandon their children. I love my own so much.' *The Princess of Wales*

'Suddenly you find that your child is not a malleable being or an offprint of you; it is the culmination of heaven knows how many thousands of years and genetic traits of your ancestors.' *Prince Charles*

'I wouldn't have missed being present when William and Harry were born. Husbands who turn up later only see a baby which might have been picked off a supermarket shelf for all they know.' *Prince Charles*

To a girlfriend:
'If I have another son and you have another daughter, we'll swap.' *The Princess of Wales*

'I love William and Harry dearly, but sometimes I just have to get away from home to get some peace.' *Prince Charles*

'Girls are so much nicer than boys, don't you think?' *Prince Charles*

'The boys are super and great fun, but I would love to have a daughter.' *Prince Charles*

'I'm not a production line, you know.' *The Princess of Wales*

'I'm too busy to have any babies for at least a year.' *The Princess of Wales*

In 1988 attention was diverted to the Duchess of York's first pregnancy.
'Both William and Harry keep asking when the baby will arrive, what he or she will be like and when they can play with him or her. They're really thrilled at all the fun they're going to have together.' *The Princess of Wales*

But after holding Princess Beatrice:
'I feel broody.' *The Princess of Wales*

'I have discovered I don't like four-year-olds.' *Prince Charles*

On the tribulations of having to lead the dance at a formal function:
'I assure you it makes the heart sink, to have to make an awful exhibition of ourselves.' *Prince Charles*

THE REAL CHARLES

'I've got a long body and short legs. And please don't blame photographers for making my ears look large. They *are* large.' *Prince Charles*

'I'm happier at home with my family than anywhere else.' *Prince Charles*

'He has no interest in things, but all the more for persons.' *Prince Philip*

'Shyness is often a disability . . . It's not only those who are confined to a wheelchair who are disabled.' *Prince Charles*

After visiting a mental hospital, asked if he had been disturbed by strange grimaces and sounds made by the inmates:
'Not really. After all, I make funny faces and funny noises from time to time. So I understand.' *Prince Charles*

'I just want to be normal.' *Prince Charles*

'Intelligent and perceptive.' *The Duke of Windsor (uncle, formerly Edward VIII)*

'If there was anything left to discover in the world, Charles would have been an explorer.' *The Queen Mother*

'What a relief it is when you find that you've actually brought up a reasonable and civilised human being.' *Prince Philip*

On weeding his favourite walled garden at Highgrove:
'Very therapeutic – weeding – and it's marvellous if you can do enough to see the effect.' *Prince Charles*

Describing himself in a television interview: 'Sometimes a bit of a twit.' *Prince Charles*

'He loves his garden, but as soon as he's finished sorting out every inch of it he will get bored with it and take up something else. He's like that.' *The Princess of Wales*

'I'm a pretty ordinary sort of person.' *Prince Charles*

'I was asked in Australia whether I concentrated on improving my image – as if I was some kind of washing powder, presumably with special blue whitener. I dare say I could improve it by growing my hair to a more fashionable length, being seen at the Playboy Club at frequent intervals and squeezing myself into excruciatingly tight clothes . . . but I intend to go on being myself to the best of my ability.' *Prince Charles*

'I am a countryman. I can't stand cities.' *Prince Charles*

'I dare say many of my views and beliefs would be considered old-fashioned and out of date, but that doesn't worry me . . . Fashion, by its very definition is transitory; human nature being what it is, what was old-fashioned at length becomes in fashion, and thus the whole process continues.' *Prince Charles*

'I like to see if I can challenge myself to do something that is potentially hazardous, just to see if mentally I can accept the challenge and carry it out . . . I'm one of those people who don't like sitting and watching someone else doing something.' *Prince Charles*

Asked what his greatest challenge had been: 'I find it quite a challenge being who I am.' *Prince Charles*

His sense of humour:
'I enjoy making people laugh. It's very useful for getting people to listen to what you are saying.' *Prince Charles*

The joke which shocked the Church in 1978: 'I hope you infants are enjoying your infancy as much as we adults are enjoying our adultery.' *Prince Charles to some schoolboys*

'I was once elected one of the world's best dressed men. The following year I was elected one of the worst dressed. At a tailor's dinner just after that I decided to have my own back. I arrived wearing white tie and tails and an old tweed jacket over the top. The British are a wonderful race – they pretended I was normally dressed.' *Prince Charles*

'It has always been one of my profoundest regrets that I was not born ten years earlier than 1948, since I would have had the pure, unbounded joy of listening avidly to the Goons each week. I only discovered that the Goon-type humour appealed to me with an hysterical totality just as the shows were drawing to a close. I discovered the "Ying Tong Song" in record form and almost at once knew it by heart – the only song I do know by heart. I plagued everybody with its dulcet tones and "Solo for A Raspberry Blower" to such an extent that when my small brothers heard a recording of the Goons for the first time, they thought it was their elder brother.' *Prince Charles*

'Were it not for my ability to see the funny side of my life, I would have been committed to an institution long ago.' *Prince Charles*

His habit of standing with his hands behind his back:
'I am often asked whether it is because of some generic trait that I stand with my hands behind, like my father. The answer is that we both have the same tailor. He makes our sleeves so tight that we can't get our hands in front.' *Prince Charles*

His friends:
'I trust my friends implicitly and they know it. The more discreet, the more trustworthy they are, the better.' *Prince Charles*

After visiting a pig farm:
'I shall become a vegetarian. I'm glad I'm not a pig.' *Prince Charles*

After seeing bare-breasted girls doing a fertility dance in Fiji:
'Well, it beats the changing of the guard, doesn't it?' *Prince Charles*

────── THE REAL DIANA ──────

'She's like a nervy racehorse. She needs careful handling.' *The Queen*

'She is a very determined young woman. I know the Royals can appear to swallow people up when others marry in and the other family always looks as if it had been pushed out, but that could never happen with us. Diana would not permit it to happen, and she always gets her way.' *Earl Spencer*

'I'd walk miles for a bacon sandwich.' *The Princess of Wales*

'I certainly feel that since I've come into public life I perhaps need a little more guidance. *The Princess of Wales*

When told by Charles to mind her head as they walked under an arch:
'Why? There's nothing in it.' *The Princess of Wales*

'If you said "Afghanistan" to Diana, she'd think it was a cheese!' *Countess Spencer*

'I like playing bridge, but I'm no good – I talk too much.' *The Princess of Wales*

'When I'm nervous I tend to giggle.' *The Princess of Wales*

About her tour to the Gulf States:
Oh, you should have seen some of those Arabs going ga-ga when they saw me on the Gulf tour. I gave them the full treatment and they were just falling all over themselves. Just turned it on and mopped them up.' *The Princess of Wales*

'Being a princess is not all it's cracked
up to be.' *The Princess of Wales*

About her first Commonwealth tour to Australia in 1983:
'It was like a baptism of fire, but by the time I left I felt I'd actually been able to achieve something.' *The Princess of Wales*

On the gruelling pace of foreign tours:
'Although you are tired you just have to get on with the job.' *The Princess of Wales*

Charles, in a letter to Diana, after she had completed her first solo foreign tour, which he signed 'Willie Wombat and I':
'We were so proud of you.' *Prince Charles*

On asking for a glass of water, during her trip to Australia:
'I'm a real Pom, the heat is getting me down.' *The Princess of Wales*

'My husband doesn't approve of the books I read.' *The Princess of Wales*

On official engagements:
'Imagine having to go to a wedding every day of your life – as the bride – well that's a bit what it's like.' *The Princess of Wales*

First reaction to Buckingham Palace staff:
'Oh everybody is so *old* around here.' *The Princess of Wales*

On the aides that surround Charles:
'It was as if he was married to them, not me, and they are so patronising it drives me mad.' *The Princess of Wales*

On being surrounded by security:
'If it's there all the time you become unconscious of it.' *The Princess of Wales*

'My husband has taught me everything I know.' *The Princess of Wales*

'The trouble with being a Princess is that it is so hard to have a pee.' *The Princess of Wales*

'I do so like men in uniform.' *The Princess of Wales*

'One of the more glamorous Colonel-in-Chiefs of the British Army.' *Prince Charles*

Diana on the phone from Kensington Palace to a friend, after the press had nicknamed her 'Disco-Di':
'It's Disco-Di from KP' *The Princess of Wales*

On wearing a portable stereo:
'I'm a great believer in having music wherever I go. And it's just a big treat to go out for a walk with music still coming with me.' *The Princess of Wales*

'She can't hear anybody coming with that contraption, you know. She just walks straight past me.' *The Queen*

Diana on the problems of drug addiction:
'We have a battle on our hands. It has to be waged on two major fronts – prevention and cure. As far as prevention is concerned, parents and teachers are in the front line. As a parent myself, I am only too aware of the responsibility this implies in terms of the kind of upbringing best suited to encourage the child to "Say No".' *The Princess of Wales*

The teetotal princess:
'One whiff of wine these days would knock me to the floor.' *The Princess of Wales*

DIANA AND APPEARANCE

'My clothes are not my priority. I enjoy bright colours and my husband likes me to look smart, presentable, but fashion isn't my big thing at all.' *The Princess of Wales*

'The Princess of Wales would look elegant in a sack.' *Princess Michael*

'You'd be amazed what one has to worry about, from the obvious things like the wind – because there is always a gale wherever we go – and the wind is my enemy, there's no doubt about that. Then you've got to put your arm up to get some flowers so you can't have anything too revealing. And you can't have hems too short because when you bend over there are six children looking up your skirt! Clothes are for the job. They've got to be practical. Sometimes I can be a little outrageous, which is quite nice. But only sometimes.' *The Princess of Wales*

'I just can't win. They either accuse me of spending too much on my clothes or of wearing the same outfit all the time. I wish everyone would stop talking about my clothes.' *The Princess of Wales*

About a Cartier watch that had taken her fancy:
'Oh it hasn't got any numbers – I couldn't manage a watch without numbers.' *The Princess of Wales*

'I don't particularly like expensive jewellery because I am frightened of losing it.' *The Princess of Wales*

'Biting one's fingernails is a hard habit to break, but I'm working on it. This is one reason I favour gloves.' *The Princess of Wales*

'I'm never on what is called a diet. Maybe I'm so scrawny because I take so much exercise . . . When I get home I just have to chase around for a chicken leg because I'm so busy.' *The Princess of Wales*

'Hats give me confidence.' *The Princess of Wales*

On plastic surgery for her nose:
'I'd love to have my conk fixed. It's too big.' *The Princess of Wales*

To a reporter who revealed she wore thermal underwear:
'I had a vision of you on your back looking up my skirt with your binoculars.' *The Princess of Wales*

Why she decided to wear a dinner jacket to a public function:
'It will amuse Charles.' *The Princess of Wales*

'When I wear a backless dress, I find that most people just don't know where to put their hands.' *The Princess of Wales*

'Various professional ladies hurl themselves without warning against one's person while one is emerging innocently from boiling surf or having executed a turn on a ski slope. All this may be harmless publicity and good for the ladies' careers, but what do you think it does to my ego?' *Prince Charles*

'I've only got to look twice at someone and the next morning I'm engaged to her.' *Prince Charles*

CHARLES AND DIANA ON LOVE AND MARRIAGE

Before Charles was married women around the world would fling themselves at him.
'I don't know how the idea got about that I am amazingly successful with women. My constant battle is to escape, and that is sometimes a very difficult thing.' *Prince Charles*

When on a tour of India in 1981 an Indian film actress asked if she could kiss him:
'Why not? Everyone else does.' *Prince Charles*

To an unknown girl who whispered to him 'You're gorgeous':
'You're spoiling me.' *Prince Charles*

In 1979:
'What I really need is a good wife.' *Prince Charles*

'I often look at someone and think, "I wonder if I could marry her?" ' *Prince Charles*

'If only I could live with a girl before marrying her, but I can't.' *Prince Charles*

On marriage:
'I'd want to marry someone whose interests I could share. A woman not only marries a man, she marries into a way of life – a job. If I'm deciding on whom I want to live with for 50 years – well, that's the last decision on which I would want my head to be ruled by my heart.' *Prince Charles*

The right age for marriage:
'30 is about the right age for a chap like me to get married.' *Prince Charles*

'When we first got married we were everyone's idea of the world's most perfect, ideal couple. Now they say we're leading separate lives. The next thing I know I'll read in some newspaper that I've got a black lover.' *The Princess of Wales*

'It's rather more than just falling madly in love with somebody and having a love affair for the rest of your married life. It's basically a very strong friendship . . . I think you are very lucky if you find the person attractive in the physical *and* mental sense . . . In many cases, you fall madly "in love" with somebody with whom you are really infatuated. To me marriage, which may be for 50 years, seems to be one of the biggest and most responsible steps to be taken in one's life.' *Prince Charles*

On choosing a suitable wife:
'I was told that before you marry the daughter you should first look at the mother.' *Prince Charles*

On being asked if he was in love with his fiancée:
'Whatever "in love" means.' *Prince Charles*

Asked the same question:
'Of course.' *Lady Diana*

On rumours of discord between them:
'The truth about our separate lives is very simple. My husband and I get around 2,000 invitations to visit different places every six months. We couldn't possibly get through many if we did them all together. This means we can get to twice as many places and see twice as many people.' *The Princess of Wales*

'People expect a great deal of us.' *Prince Charles*

One of Charles' most often-used phrases to his wife:
'Anything for a quiet life.' *Prince Charles*

'Creating a secure family unit in which to bring up children, to give them a happy secure upbringing – that is what marriage is all about.' *Prince Charles*

'I get so angry when I read something about me or my wife which is untrue, that I want to ring up the editor and complain, and I'd spend all my time on the telephone, so I've just stopped reading the other newspapers [except for the *Times*]. If I don't know what they're saying I can't get angry.' *Prince Charles*

CHARLES ON THE MONARCHY AND HIS ROLE

'The oldest profession in the world.' *Prince Charles*

On the ceremonial aspects:
'I would change nothing. Besides ceremony being a major and important aspect of monarchy, something that has grown and developed over a thousand years in Britain, I happen to enjoy it enormously.' *Prince Charles*

What he would like to change:
'The old remote image of Royalty.' *Prince Charles*

On the idea of the Queen abdicating in his favour:
'I don't think monarchs should retire and be pensioned off, say at 60. Take Queen Victoria. In her 80s she was more loved, more known, more revered in her country than she'd ever been before.' *Prince Charles*

'I've never used the phrase "When I become King" – it's so pompous.' *Prince Charles*

About the Royal Family's wealth:
'The Royal Family must have money. If they have to look to the State for everything, they become nothing more than puppets and prisoners in their own countries. That's what happened to the Japanese Royal Family.' *Prince Charles*

'There isn't any power, but there can be influence. The influence you have is in direct proportion to the respect people have for you.' *Prince Charles*

'Ich Dien', 'I serve', is the motto of the Prince of Wales.
' "I serve" is a marvellous motto to have. If you have a sense of duty, and I like to think I have, then service is something that you give to people, particularly if they want you – but sometimes if they don't.' *Prince Charles*

'I am, at best, nothing more than a travelling ambassador for Britain.' *Prince Charles*

'I am used to being regarded as an anachronism. In fact, I am coming round to think it is rather grand.' *Prince Charles*

'You can't understand what it's like to have your whole life mapped out for you a year in advance. It's so awful to be programmed. I know what I'll be doing next week, next month, even next year. At times I get so fed up with the whole idea.' *Prince Charles*

'There is no set-out role for me. It depends entirely what I make of it . . . I'm really rather an awkward problem.' *Prince Charles*

'I am heir to the throne. Full stop. That is all. I could do absolutely nothing if I wanted to. I could go and play polo all over the world.' *Prince Charles*

'I work bloody hard right now and will continue to.' *Prince Charles*

'I can't affect things on a large scale. The only way I can see myself achieving anything is by example.' *Prince Charles*

'What I have to do for England!' *Prince Charles*

'I can only go muddling along pursuing the sort of things I think are right and true, and hope there's a result. I'm not somebody overburdened with a sense of self-confidence about such things. I always feel that I should be somewhat reticent, otherwise you end up thinking you are more important than you are. I just go on trying to encourage, to help.' *Prince Charles*

'I have come to the conclusion that basically I ought to keep my mouth shut during any election campaign.' *Prince Charles*

'I have been brought up to have an active role. I am determined not to be confined to cutting ribbons.' *Prince Charles*

'I like to stir things up, to throw a proverbial royal brick through the plate glass of pompous professional pride and jump feet first into the kind of spaghetti bolognaise which clogs this country from one end to the other.' *Prince Charles*

—— CHARLES AND SPORT ——

When Charles learnt to ski, to his father:
'I've got one sport you haven't now.'

Prince Philip, to the players teaching Charles the game of polo:
'Let him have it hot and strong. Be frank and fearless.'

'I feel a hundred times better after a game of polo.' *Prince Charles*

'I wish I had been born Bob Geldof.' *Prince Charles*

Charles's statement after the skiing tragedy at Klosters in 1988, when his close friend, Major Hugh Lindsay, was killed by an avalanche:
'I would like to emphasise that all members of my party including myself were skiing off the piste at our own risk and we all accepted and always have done that mountains have to be treated with the greatest respect and not treated lightly.' *Prince Charles*

'To my horror Major Lindsay and Mrs Palmer-Tomkinson were swept away in a whirling maelstrom as the whole mountainside seemed to hurtle past us into the valley below. It was all over in a terrifying matter of seconds.' *Prince Charles*

On watching racing:
'I'd rather be riding the horses myself.' *Prince Charles*

'If I didn't get the exercise – or have something to take my mind off things – I would go potty.' *Prince Charles*

On steeplechasing:
'It's a great challenge to try to overcome a certain element of natural fear . . . going flat over fences and wondering if you are going to get to the other side in one piece.' *Prince Charles*

About the press being ever-present:
'The only time I worry when they are around is when I'm up at Balmoral fishing. When I'm standing in the river for hours I sometimes have a pee in the water. And I'm always petrified some cameraman is going to catch me at it.' *Prince Charles*

'All the newspapers seem to be interested in are pictures of me falling off a horse or having a girl fling her arms round my neck. You'd think it was the only thing I ever did.' *Prince Charles*

CHARLES AND DIANA
ON THE PRESS

'It's when nobody wants to write about you or take photographs of you that you ought to worry in my sort of job.' *Prince Charles*

An ode Charles wrote for the pressmen who were following him, to the tune of 'Immortal, Invisible'. He sang it to them, with backing from his equerry, private secretary and detective.
'Impossible, unapproachable, God only knows,
The light's always dreadful and he won't damn-well pose.
Most maddening, most curious, he simply can't fail
It's always the same with the old Prince of Wales.

Insistent, persistent, the Press never end.
One day they will drive me right round the bend.
Recording, rephrasing, every word that I say.
It's got to be news at the end of the day.

Disgraceful, most dangerous to share the same plane,
Denies me that chance to scratch and complain.
Oh where may I ask you is the monarchy going
When Princes and pressmen are in the same Boeing?' *Prince Charles*

Having tasted tea and spat into a spittoon, Charles pre-empted tabloid headlines:
'It's got to be my spitting image.' *Prince Charles*

'As I get older, I find less privacy becomes available and more people seem to be interested in every small and minute aspect of one's life. Somehow you have to have the outlook or philosophy which enables you to bear it, otherwise, I promise you, it's very easy to go mad.' *Prince Charles*

To a journalist, about another writer's article that said he had a squint:
'Liked your piece on Sunday. But did you see the *Sunday Telegraph*? I knew my eyes were close together, but not as close as that.' *Prince Charles*

On the attempts of the press to marry him off:
'I have read so many reports recently telling everyone who I am about to marry that when last year a certain young lady was staying at Sandringham a crowd of about 10,000 appeared when we went to church. Such was the obvious conviction that what they had read was true that I almost felt I had better espouse myself at once so as not to disappoint too many people.' *Prince Charles*

Sympathy for the press:
'I look at it from a newspaperman's point of view: he's got a job to do – I've got a job to do. At times they happen to coincide, and compromise must occur, otherwise misery can so easily ensue. I try to put myself in their shoes, and I hope they try to put themselves in mine, although I appreciate that is difficult.' *Prince Charles*

Offered a bouquet by photographers while on her honeymoon at Balmoral:
'I suppose that came out of your expenses.' *The Princess of Wales*

'I should like to take this opportunity to wish you all a very happy New Year and your editors a particularly nasty one.' *Prince Charles*

The Queen complaining to pressmen about their harassment of Diana:
The Queen: 'My daughter-in-law can't even go into a shop to buy winegums because of you.'
Journalist: 'Can't she send a servant to buy them?'
The Queen: 'That, if you don't mind me saying so, is an extremely pompous remark to make.'

'I simply treat the press as though they were children.' *The Princess of Wales*

'You know everything about me except how many fillings I've got. And I'm not telling you *that*.' *The Princess of Wales*

Diana in tears when she discovered a hidden photographer had caught her joking with friends – male and female – at a private house:
'I've been working hard all week. Katie fixed up a nice evening for me. She laid this whole thing on. It's very sweet and it's the only time I've been out all week. I've got so few friends left and this will only make things worse for me.' *The Princess of Wales*

When the press started criticising Diana:
'The moment people have put you on a pedestal, along comes a separate brigade that likes knocking you off. It's human nature.' *Prince Charles*

Why he won't watch programmes on Sky:
'I imagine it's a bit like watching the *Sun* on video.' *Prince Charles*

CHARLES ON CONSERVATION AND FARMING

'The supporters of organic farming, bio-agriculture, alternative agriculture and optimum production are beginning to make themselves heard . . . essential if our planet is to feed the teeming millions of people who will live on it by the 21st century.' *Prince Charles*

'We thought the world belonged to us. Now we are beginning to realise that we belong to the world. We are responsible to it *and* to each other. Our creativity is a blessing, but unless we control it, it will be our destruction.' *Prince Charles*

'Like the sorcerer's apprentice causing havoc in his master's home when he couldn't control the spell which he had released, mankind runs a similar risk of laying waste his earthly home by thinking he's in control when he's clearly not.' *Prince Charles*

On the Greenhouse Effect and beyond:
'If we can stop the sky turning into a microwave oven, we still face the prospect of living in a garbage dump.' *Prince Charles*

About his garden:
'I just come to talk to the plants, really. It's very important to talk – they respond, don't they?' *Prince Charles*

— CHARLES ON SOCIETY —

'I am not in favour of an elite if it is solely based on birth and wealth, but I am certainly in favour if it is based on high standards.' *Prince Charles*

'I believe that we should all have the opportunity at one stage in our lives to make a contribution to our community. It is also vital that we find ways in which people from all walks of life and backgrounds can operate together for a period in their lives. Ours is one of the very few countries where this does not happen.' *Prince Charles*

'I've learnt a lot, I've looked a lot, I can't just sit there and do nothing about it.' *Prince Charles*

'I think I'm becoming more eccentric as I get older.' *Prince Charles*

'Children are naturally aware, but our whole educational pattern is one where we knock it out of everybody's lives. We are a "left-brain" society, we concentrate on organising the denial of the intuitive half.' *Prince Charles*

'It's very difficult if you leave school at sixteen. I wouldn't have known what the hell to do with myself at sixteen.' *Prince Charles*

'Do we have to tolerate an incessant menu of utterly gratuitous violence on both cinema and television? . . . Those of us with children are very concerned by the appalling lack of restraint shown by those who make such films and videos, and define their so-called art by insisting on the absolute necessity of portraying real life.' *Prince Charles*

CHARLES ON SPIRITUALITY

'I rather feel that deep in the soul of mankind there is a reflection as on the surface of a mirror or a mirror-calm lake, of the beauty and harmony of the universe. We must develop an awareness of this to attain inner peace and world peace.' *Prince Charles*

'We have lost that sense of meaning within nature's scheme of things which helps to preserve that delicate balance between the world of the instinctive unconscious and that of the conscious. If we did but know it, so many of the things we feel, as it were unconsciously, are things we share, but which seem to become trapped within us through that fear of being thought different or odd.' *Prince Charles*

'I'm not interested in the occult or any of these things. I'm purely interested in being open-minded.' *Prince Charles*

Teasing his critics:
'Here I am robed, sandalled, shaven-headed and with a rather faraway look in my eyes.' *Prince Charles*

About all his supposed gurus:
'If I sat at these people's feet as often as disciples are supposed to do, I would never manage to do anything else and would probably end up developing architectural haemorrhoids.' *Prince Charles*

CHARLES ON ARCHITECTURE

'A large number of us have developed a feeling that architects tend to design for the approval of fellow architects and critics – not for the tenants.' *Prince Charles*

About the Mansion Square project:
'It would be a tragedy if the character and skyline of our capital city were to be further ruined and St Paul's dwarfed by yet another glass stump.' *Prince Charles*

About the proposed extension to the National Gallery:
'It is like a kind of vast municipal fire station . . . Like a monstrous carbuncle on the face of a much-loved and elegant friend.' *Prince Charles*

'Why on earth do we have to be surrounded by buildings that look like machines?' *Prince Charles*

THE REAL PRINCE WILLIAM —— AND PRINCE HARRY ——

William as a toddler:
'Quite a handful.' *The Princess of Wales*

'He's getting angrier and noisier by the day.' *Prince Charles*

'He's a very independent child surrounded by a tremendous amount of grownups, so his conversation is very forthright.' *The Princess of Wales*

At nursery school, to the other children:
'My daddy is the Prince of Wales and he can beat up your daddy.' *Prince William*

Prince William was chosen to be one of the bridal attendants at the wedding of the Duke and Duchess of York, and his mother was nervous about the way he would behave.
'I'm going to put down a line of Smarties in the aisle of Westminster Abbey so that William will know where to stand – and he's got to stay there . . . He's terribly excited. I only hope he behaves in the Abbey. He will rise to the occasion – at least I hope he will.' *The Princess of Wales*

After the ceremony:
'I'm glad he behaved himself, because he can be a bit of a prankster.' *The Princess of Wales*

'They are normal little boys, who are unlucky enough to create an abnormal amount of attention.' *Prince Charles*

'They are little minxes.' *The Princess of Wales*

When confronted with Bob Geldof, who was visiting Prince Charles to discuss world famine:
'Why do you talk to that man? He's all dirty. He's got scruffy hair and wet shoes.' *Prince William*

'I have to watch what I say in front of Prince William. He's so quick on the uptake that he copies everything.' *The Princess of Wales*

'I always feel he will be all right because he has been born to his royal role. He will get accustomed to it gradually.' *The Princess of Wales*

When asked by a classmate at nursery school what prep school he would be going to:
'I don't know. I'm not allowed to know 'cos of security.' *Prince William*

'Wills' and 'The Tornado'. *Family nicknames for William*

'William is the greatest possible fun. He's a most enjoyable child, but then one always thinks one's own child is.' *Prince Charles*

'William is a proper little gentleman. He opens doors for women and calls men "sir".' *The Princess of Wales*

Talking about his first pony, Whisky, to his startled nursery school teacher:
'Whisky is such fun!' *Prince William*

William was disappointed when, on his second day at Wetherby School, he wasn't greeted by the same horde of reporters who had been waiting for him on his first day.
Prince William: 'Where have all the photographers gone?'
Princess of Wales: 'Don't be so grand, William.'

'William is just like me – always in trouble.' *The Princess of Wales*

Of William and Harry:
'Harry is the mischievous one.' *The Princess of Wales*

What they eat:
'I'm afraid they'd rather eat the things that are bad for them, just like all children.' *The Princess of Wales*

On settling arguments between the boys and their nanny:
'I always listen to both sides of an argument, then make my decision.' *The Princess of Wales*

5

THE PRINCESS ROYAL
&
HER FAMILY

'It's the sweetest girl!' *Prince Philip*

About his baby daughter who gurgled all the time:
'We have a budding opera singer in the family.' *Prince Philip*

On being told the names of the new Princess:
'Unusual and charming.' *George VI*

The first official photographs were taken by Cecil Beaton, who described his impressions of Princess Anne:
'A small baby with quite a definite nose for one so young, large, sleepy, grey-green eyes and a particularly pretty mouth.' *Cecil Beaton*

PRINCESS ANNE

Princess Anne Elizabeth Alice Louise was born on the morning of 15 August 1950, weighing six pounds. The first and only daughter of the Duke and Duchess of Edinburgh – Princess Elizabeth and Prince Philip – was born two years after her elder brother, and was third in line to the throne. She was blue-eyed and blonde-haired.

During the photo session Prince Charles suddenly decided to join in, and a picture was taken of him kissing his baby sister on the cheek. His mother was delighted:
'It's delicious – most fortunate in every way!' *Princess Elizabeth*

Princess Anne was nearly eighteen months old when her mother became Queen, and shortly afterwards the family moved into Buckingham Palace. The Queen was crowned when Anne was not quite three, and considered too young to attend the ceremony. She remembered:

'The normal sisterly fury at being left behind.' *Princess Anne*

Soon Anne was taking lessons with Charles under the care of their governess, Miss Peebles.

'She started with my brother and I went along, I suppose, none of which I fortunately remember.' *Princess Anne*

On her relationship with Charles:

'We fought like cats and dogs... Having an elder brother, I was rather more interested in playing the sort of games that he was playing, rather than anything else... I am delighted that I did not have a sister.' *Princess Anne*

On Charles' relationship with the Queen Mother:

'There is rather a special relationship between the eldest grandson and a grandmother, I think, which is not true of grand-daughters.' *Princess Anne*

On her first riding lessons with Charles:

'We were both on a leading rein and we were *towed* around a cinder ring, but the fastest we ever went was a trot. I'm afraid I thought it was a grisly waste of time.' *Princess Anne*

Now that Anne's mother was Queen she seemed to be always travelling. Anne and Charles were looked after in her absence by nannies and governesses. The Queen, who missed both her children badly while she was away, commissioned a drawing of Anne by the artist Ulrica Forbes, who described the little girl:

'The most appealingly friendly child, small yet tall for her age, shaking my

Anne was bought her first pony, William, when she was three years old.

'I grew up with ponies... Horses were always around.' *Princess Anne*

hand with a surprisingly firm grip.' *Ulrica Forbes*

At one point Charles entered the room.
Ulrica Forbes (to his nanny): 'Isn't he b-e-a-u-t-i-f-u-l?'
Prince Charles: 'I *can* spell you know.'
Princess Anne (eagerly): 'Yes! He can spell Jack!'

Just after her fifth birthday Anne started to have proper lessons at Buckingham Palace, with two other girls of her age. One day, Miss Peebles 'Mispy', took them to the Planetarium, and when they came out they saw a queue of children waiting to be let in.
Small boy in the crowd: 'What's the show like?'
Princess Anne: 'It was wonderful!' (then anxiously to Mispy) 'That's what Mummy would have said, isn't it?'

'I've always accepted the role of being second in everything from quite an early age. You adopt that position as part of your experience. You start off in life very much a tail-end Charlie, at the back of the line.' *Princess Anne*

Anne was once furious when Prince Philip took Charles out sailing, but said that she could not come because she was too young – Charles was two years older.
'Really only two inches taller!' *Princess Anne*

'Perhaps I did spoil her at times.' *Prince Philip*

═══════════════════════════

Prince Andrew was born in February 1960, when Anne was nine. She had hoped for a baby brother and was thrilled. She was shortly to act as bridesmaid to Aunt Margo, Princess Margaret, but was more interested in the new baby than in being fitted for bridesmaids' dresses.
'Anne's so busy pram-pushing, we must hope she can find the time!' *Princess Margaret*

═══════════════════════════

Anne was bossy and authoritative with her younger brother, and with Prince Edward, who was born in 1964.
'I couldn't help being big sister with that sort of gap in age – because you know that you always consider that they're not always getting the sort of discipline you got when you were small.' *Princess Anne*

═══════════════════════════

On family life:
'As a child and up to my teens, I don't think I went along with the family bit, not until later than anyone else. I know its value now, but I don't think I did up to my middle teens.' *Princess Anne*

═══════════════════════════

Anne always loved horses, and first competed in a riding competition when she was eleven, riding Bandit, the pony she shared with Prince Charles. She was given her own pony, High Jinks, for her twelfth birthday. She started to enter competitions and won quite a few – including a silver challenge cup for the best under-thirteen rider in a field of twenty.
Anne had always envied the fact that Prince Charles went to school, while she had to be content with a governess, but at the age of thirteen she became a boarder at Benenden school. Her first impression was of:
'The continuous noise and the fact that everywhere you turned there were so many people.' *Princess Anne*

'Noise and smells – that's what school meant to me – cabbage and polish.' *Princess Anne*

Approving verdict on her schoolmates:
'A caustic lot who knew exactly what they thought about other people and saved one a lot of embarrassment.' *Princess Anne*

Anne loved school, unlike Charles, who had found it an ordeal. After an afternoon away:
'Do you think I can get back early?' *Princess Anne*

She found it all great fun. She wrote about one party at school:
'The Hall had been valiantly disguised à la Bonnie and Clyde, making a bar manned by dollies with maxi-skirts, bright red lipsticks, horizontal headbands and those shoes! The rest of us were ordered to wear necklaces – dresses not needed!' *Princess Anne*

On pocket money at school:
'We had two [pounds] a term and as I had been brought up by a careful Scots nanny to appreciate the value of money, I simply didn't spend my allotment. I've always been mean with money and as far as I know, I was the only girl in the school who had any left at the end of term.' *Princess Anne*

'I gave up hockey as soon as possible and I didn't like netball because I used to get wolf whistles in my short skirt! I was a bit of a softie and I didn't like rough games.' *Princess Anne*

Anne continued to ride at a school close to Benenden. She was one of the more advanced riders, and sometimes her impatience got the better of her.
'She took a mischievous delight in disrupting her class at intervals by pinching Jinks behind the saddle so that he bucked!' *One of the instructors*

Once Anne had a part in a school play, which involved her riding. The school insisted that she wore a hard hat under her feathered Tudor bonnet. Anne was convinced that she would look ridiculous.
Princess Anne: 'I won't do it – I'll phone Mummy!'
The Queen: 'If you've been told to wear a cap, you jolly well will have to wear a cap!'

How the other girls reacted to her:
'They accept people for what they are rather quicker than adults do. They have no preconceived ideas, because how could they have?' *Princess Anne*

Anne was most concerned to fit in with the other girls, and was nervous when her parents turned up and she was made to feel different. She made jokes to guard against being teased. Once she was collected by car to lunch with the Archbishop of Canterbury:
'Watch my halo!' *Princess Anne*

In 1968, her last year of school, Anne became Captain of House. She passed 'A' levels in History and Geography, with a special Merit in an optional extra Geography paper.
'She was a good monitor and later a very capable Captain of House who was able to exert her authority in a natural manner without being aggressive. If there was any failing at all it was possibly her impatience. She was extremely quick to grasp things herself and couldn't understand anyone else not being able to do so.' *The headmistress*

On why she didn't want to go to university:
'I think it's a very much over-rated pastime.' *Princess Anne*

1968 saw the Mexican Olympics, when Britain's Three-Day Event team won the gold medal for the second time. Anne went with the Queen Mother to a cocktail party to honour the riders, where she met the young reserve rider, Mark Phillips, for the first time. They did not – then – strike up a friendship, but the press were already wondering about Anne's marriage prospects.
'Princesses are getting a bit short in the market. I'll soon be next – but they'll have a hard job marrying me off to someone I don't want. I'll marry the man I choose, no matter who he is or what he does.' *Princess Anne*

After her trip to New York with Prince Charles in 1969, where the verdict was that she was 'sullen, ungracious and plain bored':
'Every time I turn round 20 million reporters are on my heels, and I can't get used to it.' *Princess Anne*

As their Colonel-in-Chief, Anne paid a visit to the 14th/20th King's Hussars in 1970, during which she drove a Chieftain tank.

'I'd love one for Christmas!' *Princess Anne*
(But what she got was a diamond brooch and the number plates 1420H for her car.)
In the same year she joined her mother on a tour of Australia. The Australian press complained that she did not smile enough.
'It's difficult to keep the smile bright when you're fourth in line.' *Princess Anne*

In January 1971 Anne became President of The Save The Children Fund.
'You don't have to be crazy about children to want to give them a better start in life.' *Princess Anne*

Later in 1971 she and Charles made a film on the Fund's work in Kenya for the children's programme Blue Peter. *She was a natural in front of the cameras.*
'We hadn't been filming a couple of minutes before we knew that if the film was a flop it wouldn't be Princess Anne's fault.' *The producer*

Anne was becoming more and more ambitious in her riding, and in April 1971 she qualified for the Badminton Three-Day Event. Some people said she would barely be able to keep up, and that she would come near last – but her riding coach Alison Oliver knew better: 'She is so mad keen that she never tires of practice, practice and more practice. Some experts say she is a stylish rider, but I think workmanlike is a better description. She has determination plus a load of guts.' *Alison Oliver*

Anne, riding Doublet, came in fifth out of 48 – Mark Phillips was the outright winner. 'She rode the course in a way which I can only describe as innocent. There was a delight to her riding which was fresh and enthusiastic which was absolutely rare in competition at that level. She appeared to be enjoying herself all the way around and she was a joy to watch. Even though she was ambitious even at that stage, there wasn't apparent the sometimes bitter single-mindedness that characterizes so many of the world's leading sportsmen.' *Alison Oliver*

Because of her performance at Badminton Anne was invited to compete in the European Championships as an individual alongside the British team. Despite having to go to hospital for an operation on an ovarian cyst, Anne was determined to accept and to recover fully for the event. The result was better than anyone hoped: Great Britain won the team championship and Princess Anne won the European individual gold medal.

Anne now had her eye on doing even better at Badminton in 1972, but Doublet bruised a tendon and she had to withdraw. She went along as a spectator anyway, and this is when her friendship with Mark Phillips took a new turn.

'What singles her out as a competitor is her burning desire to be in the winner's enclosure.' *Alison Oliver*

CAPTAIN MARK PHILLIPS

Mark Phillips was born in September 1948. His father Peter Phillips rose to the rank of Major in the Army and then left to go into business. Mark's mother Anne was the daughter of a brigadier who was an aide-de-camp to George VI. Mark was a shy little boy, and at Marlborough, the public school he attended, he was thought to be modest, hard-working and pleasant. Like his father he entered the army – joining the Royal Greenjackets. Afterwards he won a commission in the Queen's Dragoon Guards.

Mark was always a talented rider and had been competing and winning in horse trials since 1967. He was a member of the British Olympic Team in 1972, and it was their love of horses and riding skills which brought Anne and Mark together. From Badminton onwards, the two began seeing a lot of each other:
'The press would be surprised how often we have been out to dinner and they haven't noticed it.' *Captain Mark Phillips*

THE ENGAGEMENT
AND WEDDING

The romance with Mark Phillips was flourishing so it was inevitable that the press would finally get wind of it. Anne and Mark tried to put reporters off the scent.
'Princess Anne and I are just good friends with a common interest and great love of horses.' *Captain Mark Phillips*

'He's very, very strong – horses rarely stop with him and if they do they wish they hadn't.' *Princess Anne*

'I can't understand why there has been all this interest in our riding together. Lieutenant Phillips has been coming here solely to exercise the horse he is riding at Badminton, which is stabled here and belongs to the Queen.' *Princess Anne*

Knowing this was not true the press kept closer to Anne than ever before, following her everywhere.
'I don't know why I am being subjected to this nonsensical treatment. This is what raises my blood pressure.' *Princess Anne*

Once they decided that they wanted to marry, Mark told his mother:
Mrs Anne Phillips: 'What's her name?'
Captain Mark Phillips: 'Princess Anne.'
Mrs Anne Phillips (deathly pause): 'You must be joking!'
Captain Mark Phillips: 'No I'm absolutely serious.'

On 29 May 1973 this announcement appeared in the Court Circular:
'It is with the greatest pleasure that the Queen and the Duke of Edinburgh announce the betrothal of their beloved daughter the Princess Anne to Lieutenant Mark Phillips, the Queen's Dragoon Guards, son of Mr and Mrs Peter Phillips.'

'People don't believe when we say that in March we had no intention of getting married. In fact it is absolutely true and it was only after Badminton [in April] . . . that it seemed like a good idea.' *Princess Anne*

'He kept telling me he was a confirmed bachelor and I thought at least one knows where one stands. I mean, I wasn't thinking about it.' *Princess Anne*

'They could almost have been computer dated.' *The Queen Mother*

'I'd prefer a quiet wedding, but the Queen wants Westminster Abbey.' *Princess Anne*

Just before the wedding Mark was promoted from Lieutenant to Captain – but was not offered a title by the Queen, as neither he nor Anne wished for one.

'There was no reason why Mark should be given a title when we married. He was never going to take part in public duties in his own right, so the question didn't arise.' *Princess Anne*

They were married on 14 November 1973, which happened to be Prince Charles's 25th birthday, at Westminster Abbey.

'Every day people pick up the paper and read about some disaster – I think they are rather relieved to read about something that is genuinely happy and good.' *Captain Mark Phillips*

Anne only wanted two bridal attendants: her youngest brother, Prince Edward, and her cousin, Lady Sarah Armstrong-Jones, both of them nine years old. It was partly because she had bad memories of being a bridesmaid herself, and did not want to be followed down the aisle by:

'Hordes of uncontrollable children.' *Princess Anne*

Asked by her father as they walked down the aisle whether she was nervous:
'No, of course not.' *Princess Anne*

Asked what he hoped for the future:
'A certain amount of privacy that we may be allowed to have a private life.' *Captain Mark Phillips*

Asked if Anne's Royal status had put him off:
'If that thought had stopped me marrying the person I loved it wouldn't have been much of a relationship – we both loved each other.' *Captain Mark Phillips*

To a French visitor about the French press, a few months after her marriage:
'Am I divorced yet?' *Princess Anne*

After the wedding Mark became an instructor at Sandhurst, and they moved into Oak Grove House nearby rather than the usual army quarters. In every other way they tried to be the same as the other officers and wives.
'Princess Anne and Mark set out deliberately to join the normal mess life of the college and they refused point blank to give dinner parties exclusively for the senior officers . . . If we were getting together for a few drinks, or in her case the inevitable Coca-Cola, we found that one of her favourite places for sitting was on the floor.' *Malcolm McVittie, a fellow officer*

They had no immediate plans to have children.
'Having a family can wait a bit longer. I know that some people think you should have your children sooner rather than later, when you are closer in age, but I am not sure. My own family is a splendid example of inconsistency. There was one lot when my mother was very young and a second lot later on. But I don't think you are settled enough at the beginning of your marriage to have children.' *Princess Anne*

In the evening of 20 March 1974 Anne and Mark were driving back from a film preview to Buckingham Palace with three other people when their car was brought to a halt by another car and an armed man tried to drag Anne from the car. When she asked him what he wanted her for, he said, 'I'll get a couple of million.' He shot her bodyguard Inspector Beaton in the chest and then in the hand and stomach, firing wildly into the car. Passers-by came to help, and before the gunman was disarmed he had shot two other men in the chest and a policeman in the stomach.

Attempting to bring the gunman to his senses:
'If you stop now, we'll say no more about it.' *Princess Anne*

'We are very thankful to be in one piece. But we are deeply disturbed and concerned about those who got injured, including our chauffeur and Inspector Beaton. Inspector Beaton acted particularly bravely and although already shot he continued to protect us. We are extremely grateful to all those members of the police and public who tried to help us.' *Princess Anne's official statement*

'My first reaction was anger. I was furious at this man who was having a tug-of-war with me. He ripped my dress which was a favourite blue velvet I had had made specially to wear away on honeymoon, but of course our main concern was for the people who tried to save us and who had been shot. They were very brave and looking back on it now their actions seem even more courageous when you think about them in the cold light of day.' *Princess Anne*

'If the man had succeeded in abducting Anne she would have given him a hell of a time while in captivity.' *Prince Philip*

How the attempt has affected her since:
'The difference now is that when I am on 'walkabout" I think and act like a policeman – my eyes are everywhere.' *Princess Anne*

In September 1976 the couple became the owners of Gatcombe Park in Gloucestershire, which the Queen bought for them. Mark left the Army so that he could run the estate.

'I expect their children will be four-legged.' *The Queen*

'It's nice to think I've done something right for a change.' *Captain Mark Phillips*

Anne was pregnant with her first child.
'Being pregnant is an occupational hazard of being a wife.' *Princess Anne*

The house was ready for them to move into at the time Anne was ready to give birth.
'We did the thing you should never do, have a baby and move house at the same time.' *Princess Anne*

On 15 November 1977 Anne gave birth to a son at St Mary's Hospital Paddington – the first royal baby to be born a commoner for 500 years. Mark was present at the birth.
To her husband:
'Honestly, three-day eventing at Burghley is a doddle compared to this.' *Princess Anne*

The Queen had been about to hold an investiture when the call came through from Mark that Anne had given birth. As a result the Queen was a few minutes late.
'I apologise for being late but I have just had a message from the hospital. My daughter has just given birth to a son.' *The Queen*

The baby was christened Peter Mark Andrew on 22 December. Anne was concerned that he should not have to live his life in the limelight as she had done.
'On the one hand you say, "He must be allowed to live a normal life", and you try to keep him out of the limelight as much as possible. On the other hand, he has to know that it is there,

otherwise the shock when the limelight comes is going to be awful. I hope that at any rate he'll get through his school career without too much trouble . . . At the end of the day, people are always going to refer to him as "the grandson of the Queen".' *Princess Anne*

Peter was four when Anne became pregnant again. His sister was born on 15 May 1981 in the same hospital. The baby was christened Zara, meaning 'bright as the dawn': Prince Charles suggested the name.
'The baby made a somewhat positive arrival and my brother thought that Zara was an appropriate name . . . I heard from just about every Zara in Britain at the time and I promise you there are quite a few.' *Princess Anne*

On being asked what her children were like:
'I think at this stage in their careers, the less people know about them the better.' *Princess Anne*

But later she did reveal:
'My son is one of the most gregarious people I have ever met.' *Princess Anne*

THE BREAK-UP

In April 1989 rumours of discord in the marriage were brought to a head when some personal letters written to Anne were stolen and delivered to The Sun *newspaper. A police enquiry ensued to discover the identity of the thief and Buckingham Palace issued the following statement:*
'The stolen letters were addressed to the Princess Royal by Commander Timothy Laurence, the Queen's Equerry. We have nothing to say about the contents of personal letters sent to Her Royal Highness by a friend, which were stolen and which are the subject of police investigation.'

The Palace press office attacked the rumours which followed that Princess Anne was having an affair with Commander Laurence:
'Scurrilous, absurd and without foundation.'

Mark tried to quell the flurry of rumours.
'Everything between us is fine and happy.' *Captain Mark Phillips*

'What scandal? There is none.' *Captain Mark Phillips*

Mark's father, Major Peter Phillips, commented on his son's long-distance marriage:
'It's not the sort of marriage ordinary people would understand at all . . . They spend so much time away from one another. If people are royal, they do not necessarily spend lots of time together. It's inevitable.' *Major Peter Phillips*

'It is certainly not what I would want from a marriage, but it is what they have chosen.' *Major Peter Phillips*

On the way the press dealt with the matter:
'I find this a thoroughly filthy and despicable job.' *Major Peter Phillips*

During an official opening ceremony, Anne was presented with two cheques for The Save The Children Fund. After the recent press attention, she commented:
'This does something to restore one's faith in humans.' *Princess Anne*

While Princess Anne was in Puerto Rico on Olympic business, it was officially announced by Buckingham Palace on 31 August 1989 that she was to separate from her husband after fifteen years of marriage.
'Her Royal Highness the Princess Royal and Captain Mark Phillips have decided to separate on terms agreed between them. There are no plans for divorce proceedings.'

Mark had not expected the separation to be announced so soon:
'Mark was deeply shocked and had certainly not expected it.' *Major Peter Phillips*

'Her relationship with Commander Laurence played no small part in all this.' *Major Peter Phillips*

On Captain Mark Phillips:
'He will keep regularly in touch with the children.' *Major Peter Phillips*

THE REAL PRINCESS ANNE

'I'm me. I'm a person, I'm an individual, and I think it's better for everybody that I shouldn't pretend to be anything that I'm not.' *Princess Anne*

'I like to ask people what they were expecting, you see, before they met me, and then I find out what my image was.' *Princess Anne*

'One of the things you have to learn early on in our sort of life is not to feel inadequate, because you certainly don't know as much as academics, but you can always learn.' *Princess Anne*

'I am an optimist about certain things, but I am not a natural optimist.' *Princess Anne*

To a photographer who called her 'love':
'I'm not your love. I'm your Royal Highness.' *Princess Anne*

'My parents . . . warned me that some people would want to make friends because of who you were. And I think that was fair comment, and it was important to know that. Not that it only applied to us. I think I've been lucky with the friends I've got. I don't reckon I've very many good friends, but that's partly the life one leads – one doesn't stay still for terribly long.' *Princess Anne*

She prefers to entertain friends informally.
'They know they are welcome and I like people to ring up or simply drop in.' *Princess Anne*

'Economy is bred into me. I was brought up by my parents and by my nanny to believe that things were not to be wasted.' *Princess Anne*

Meeting Kate Robbins who said, 'Hello, I do an impression of your sister-in-law Sarah':
'Really? I'll bet you can't do an impression of me. Your nose isn't big enough for a start.' *Princess Anne*

'I never was a fairy-tale princess . . . I never was and I never will be.' *Princess Anne*

'I don't think a Princess is anything I ever played at really. I have probably been playing it ever since!' *Princess Anne*

'Anne's much more positive than I was. She's much tougher too: she has been brought up in a different atmosphere.' *Princess Margaret*

'I didn't match up to the public's idea of a fairy Princess in the first place! The Princess of Wales has obviously filled a void in the media's life which I had *not* filled, but I never had any intention of filling it. I had already made a decision that it wasn't me in any way.' *Princess Anne*

On newspaper reports that she doesn't get on with Diana:
'That was one of their better fairy stories.' *Princess Anne*

'I'm her biggest fan. We've always hit it off very well and I think she's marvellous.' *The Princess of Wales*

On why she was rude to photographers when they snapped her falling off a horse:
'Okay, one says things one doesn't . . . one, okay, regrets. But under the heat of the moment, I mean, one was a very disappointed person at that particular moment in time and they were all over the place.' *Princess Anne*

'I cannot remember a single occasion when she reminded us that she was a Princess, or a single occasion when she used her position to refuse an unpleasant task.' *Alison Oliver, her riding coach*

Her relationship with her mother:
'It's much more difficult to remember that she's Queen than a mother. After all, I've known her longer as a mother than as a Queen.' *Princess Anne*

'I don't drink. Nobody believes me. I drink basically coke. Maybe orange or tomato.' *Princess Anne*

On the farm:
'Anne helps by doing a bit of tractor work, unloading bales during harvest time.' *Captain Mark Phillips*

'The more you appear in public, the more there is published about you, the more you want – and need – a real honest-to-goodness *home* life in proper privacy.' *Princess Anne*

Her ideal holiday:
'A couple of weeks in Scotland and, if the family were there at the time, especially at Balmoral. Because you can do as much as you like on your own, or you can do things with other people. It suits many of your moods. And it's very beautiful.' *Princess Anne*

On AIDS:
'Some people would say the AIDS epidemic was a classic own goal inflicted by the human race on itself. It is a self-inflicted wound that only serves to remind homo sapiens of his fallibility.' *Princess Anne*

THE REAL CAPTAIN MARK PHILLIPS

On his nickname 'Captain Fog' (because he's thick and wet):
'You generally get to know about your nickname for some reason or another – but I never knew about that one until it appeared in a gossip column. No one ever *said* it to me. I think it's rather unkind.' *Captain Mark Phillips*

'When we go out to do official engagements it's Princess Anne people have come to see and speak to. I'm just there to make up the numbers and be of any help I can. But when we're at home, there is absolutely no reason why we shouldn't have a normal husband and wife relationship. And we do.' *Captain Mark Phillips*

About married life:
'We've had a few ups and down, but life's pretty good, really, in the long run. I wouldn't change anything.' *Captain Mark Phillips*

About visiting Buckingham Palace:
'I don't feel as relaxed as I do in my own home. But then I don't expect anyone does when visiting their mother-in-law.' *Captain Mark Phillips*

About Prince Charles:
'If there is any animosity, nobody has told me about it. I think we get on really well together.' *Captain Mark Phillips*

— PRINCESS ANNE'S ROLE —

On being Royal:
'The idea of opting out is a non-starter.' *Princess Anne*

'I am the Queen's daughter, and as a daughter, I get less involved than the boys. I doubt if the next generation will be involved at all.' *Princess Anne*

'If you stop having nerves, you're not doing the job as well as you should.' *Princess Anne*

'When you are doing it, you think to yourself, "*Why*? Why do I do this?" – and afterwards you realise it is well worthwhile.' *Princess Anne*

On her speeches:
'I do all my own and always have done. Writing a speech is always a chore even if you know what you are talking about, although obviously it's easier if you do.' *Princess Anne*

On sight-seeing when on tour:
'Purgatory . . . You never see anything; either too many people or too many press.' *Princess Anne*

'We've never had a holiday. A week or two at Balmoral or ten days at Sandringham is the nearest we get.' *Princess Anne*

'You can't smile all the time . . . it is difficult, I always think, to take an intelligent interest *and* wear a grin. Male members of Royalty are not expected to meet such high standards and can appear serious or distant in public without being criticised. Men can be serious. They are allowed to be.' *Princess Anne*

On the fact that she sometimes puts her timetable out by chatting too long to people at official functions:
'If they have taken the time and trouble to come and see me, the very least I can do is to spend a few moments with them, and what's more it's something I thoroughly enjoy anyway.' *Princess Anne*

On her ladies-in-waiting:
'What they have to be good at is chatting to people and making them feel comfortable because that helps me really.' *Princess Anne*

ANNE ON RIDING

'It's the one thing that the world can see I can do well that's got *nothing* whatever to do with my position, or money, or anything else. If I'm good at it, I'm good at it – and not because I'm Princess Anne.' *Princess Anne*

On when to give up:
'When you lose your nerve. It shouldn't take long.' *Princess Anne*

On the money she gets from the civil list:
'I never have, and never will, spend a single penny of it on horses.' *Princess Anne*

Why she feels so good on a horse:
'I reckon I found the answer in this piece of information pertaining to the Amazons, those formidable forerunners to the Women's Liberation Movement with whom, incidentally, I have no sympathy. They were, apparently, at their most formidable on horseback.' *Princess Anne*

On her horsey image:
'When I appear in public people expect me to neigh, grind my teeth, paw the ground and swish my tail.' *Princess Anne*

When one of her favourite horses, Doublet, had to be put down:
'It was quite the most ghastly experience of my entire life.' *Princess Anne*

'There's a moment in sport when the enjoyment wears off because of the pressure put on you to be successful. That is the moment to stop and make sure in your own mind what sport is all about.' *Princess Anne*

'When I'm approaching a water-jump with dozens of photographers waiting for me to fall in, and hundreds of spectators wondering what's going to happen next, the horse is just about the only one who doesn't know I'm Royal.' *Princess Anne*

'If I wasn't who I am, I would like to be a lorry driver.' *Princess Anne*

——ANNE ON CLOTHES——

When her clothes were being admired:
'It's always a total mystery to me why I am described as a fashion leader. Clothes are part of the job – if you can call it a job.' *Princess Anne*

When her clothes were being criticised:
'People say one's a bit square. Well, fine – I've never pretended to be anything else.' *Princess Anne*

About 'hot pants':
'Hot pants are the limit. People complain you are not with it, but certain things I will not do.'

'I hate spending money on expensive shoes.' *Princess Anne*

'Following the fashion is very restricting; if you really follow fashion you have to get new clothes every year. And I'm not one for that. I've had clothes I've had for years, and I intend going on wearing them because I like them. I liked them when I bought them and I like them now – more so, perhaps.' *Princess Anne*

'As I get older I'm becoming more adventurous not only in my clothes but also what I eat.' *Princess Anne*

How she keeps slim:
'Eating all my favourite foods but only half what I really want.' *Princess Anne*

——— ANNE ON THE PRESS ———

On her early, unfavourable image:
'When you're a youngster practically everything you do is wrong in terms of your ability to fit in with people. You don't know enough, you don't quite know what you want to do in life.' *Princess Anne*

When the press suddenly decided she was a 'good thing' after her gruelling Save The Children Fund tour in 1982:
'I did notice my miraculous transformation.' *Princess Anne*

'It's nice when one reads something pleasant.' *Princess Anne*

'If the press can be so wrong, so trivial and so irresponsible about the Royal family, the subject I know most about, then they may be wrong, trivial, irresponsible, etc about everything else.' *Princess Anne*

'I stand somewhere to the right of Genghis Khan in my attitude to the press. Alfred the Great in the ninth century took a stronger line. Persistent slanderers had their tongues cut out.' *Princess Anne*

To a reporter, who said it was lovely to see her again:
'Oh really, why?' *Princess Anne*

On reading something unpleasant about herself:
'If it is completely untrue then it doesn't hurt at all because, in a way, it doesn't matter.' *Princess Anne*

'The press must think I'm very strange. But this does not particularly worry me.' *Princess Anne*

'They are always waiting for me to put my foot in it just like my father.' *Princess Anne*

When photographers tried to persuade her to pose for pictures:
'I don't do stunts.' *Princess Anne*

'I don't think children came into my original thoughts about it, not necessarily because I like children – if you've got two small brothers that isn't the first thing that enters your head.' *Princess Anne*

ANNE ON THE SAVE
— THE CHILDREN FUND —

'The fund offered me the chance of a Presidency with a *working* life, a chance to do more.' *Princess Anne*

'As President . . . one of the few things I suppose I can achieve is publicity.' *Princess Anne*

'I decided right from the start that if I was going to become involved with an organisation, I was going to try and do something for them, apart from just lending my name'. *Princess Anne*

'Children are very easy to feel sorry for, but they are not always so easy to be constructive about in terms of assistance.' *Princess Anne*

About the trip to Africa in 1982:
' "Wasn't it very depressing?" People ask. No. It was very encouraging – you're doing something constructive and you're doing it in the right sort of way.' *Princess Anne*

'If you don't invest in people at the earliest point of their lives you miss an opportunity – and you never get the chance again.' *Princess Anne*

'It's quite possible that I appreciate my own children more because of it.' *Princess Anne*

'I feel quite sorry for anyone silly enough to ask me if I enjoyed my trip. I give them a contemplative look to find out whether they're genuinely interested, and if it seems a polite enquiry I simply say "Yes, thank you," and leave it.' *Princess Anne*

'Survival: that's the name of the game.' *Princess Anne*

6

THE DUKE
&
DUCHESS OF YORK

── PRINCE ANDREW ──

Andrew Albert Christian Edward, third child and second son of the Queen and Prince Philip, was born on 19 February 1960, nearly ten years after his nearest sibling Princess Anne. It had been settled only a few days before his birth that he should take the surname Mountbatten-Windsor – before this the Queen's children had been Windsor only, with no reference to their father's name.

Because both the Queen and Prince Philip thought that their two elder children had suffered from being constantly in the limelight, Andrew's childhood was much more private. Since few official pictures were published and he was rarely seen, the rumour started that there was something wrong with him. Shortly after such insinuations were published in a French magazine the Queen took Andrew, aged 16 months, on to the balcony at Buckingham Palace to watch the fly-past after the Trooping the Colour in 1961. It could be seen that he was a healthy, sturdy child.

'I think children always do better if they are born with the spring and summer ahead of them.' *The Queen*

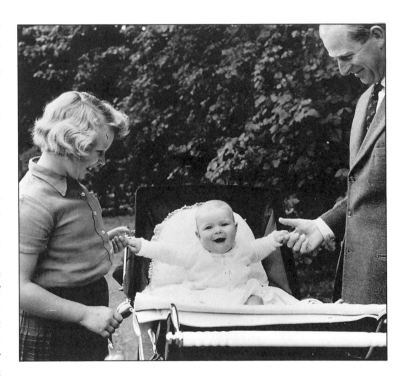

'A charmer.' *Princess Anne*

'Always full of smiles.' *Midwife Sister Rowe*

'Andy Pandy.' *Andrew's nickname by the Palace staff*

When Andrew was three the Queen Mother commissioned the sculptor Franta Belsky to make a portrait of him in bronze.
'I want it done before he loses the look of babyhood.' *The Queen Mother*

While she worked on the preliminary clay busts, Ms Belsky gave Andrew some clay.
'I have never seen such sustained concentration and excitement of discovery in a child.'

Andrew was first educated privately at Buckingham Palace. His governess was 'Mispy', who had also taught Charles and Anne. He was joined by three other boys and two girls. It was already clear that he was a 'real boy', tough and somewhat arrogant.
'A natural boss.' *Prince Philip*

'Not always a little ray of sunshine.'
The Queen

'Just wait till you go to school. Then you'll have to knuckle down.' *Prince Charles*

During the changing of the guard at Balmoral Castle, when the commander, as usual, asked the Queen's permission to march off:
'I do wish Mummy would say "No" for a change.' *Prince Andrew*

When Andrew was eight-and-a-half he was sent to Heatherdown boarding school close to Windsor Castle.

'The object is to let him lead as normal a schoolboy life as possible.' *The headmaster*

After Heatherdown Andrew followed his father and elder brother to Gordonstoun. It had changed since Charles's day – showers were no longer icy cold, and the school now accepted girl pupils.
'There was a bit of "I am the Prince" about him when he first arrived. But you can't get away with that sort of thing at Gordonstoun and it was soon knocked out of him. The ribbings he got were unmerciful and he caught on fast. He had to.' *A fellow pupil*

In 1976 Andrew, now sixteen, joined the Royal party at the Montreal Olympics, where the Canadian Prime Minister Pierre Trudeau suggested that Andrew should spend some time at school in Canada. The suggestion was accepted and Andrew started at Lakefield College School in Ontario in 1977. He was not quite seventeen when he held his first press conference there.
'This is the first time I have done this sort of thing. I'm only a nipper – not considered old enough for interviews with the press.' *Prince Andrew*

'The beds are as hard as iron. It's straw mattresses and bread and water. It's just like a prison. It may be colder in Canada but the beds are more comfortable.' *Prince Andrew*

Asked what he thought about the fact that the Canadian press had labelled him Prince Charming:
'Goodness. No comment. That's too dangerous.' *Prince Andrew*

'Girls? I like them as much as the next guy.' *Prince Andrew*

'Randy Andy.' *Andrew's nickname.*

When dancing cheek to cheek with a girl at the age of sixteen:
'If Mum could see me now, she'd wag her finger at me.' *Prince Andrew*

At Lakefield Andrew learnt to play ice hockey.
'He was pretty good. He quite surprised me. He was quite vicious too, and you need to be a bit vicious to be good at this game.' *Lakefield's head boy*

There was a school dance shortly after he arrived, and Andrew sent an invitation to a girl he had met at the Montreal Olympics, Sandi Jones, the daughter of the man who organised the Olympic yachting events.
'I was flabbergasted when I received it, although I guess we took a shine to each other when we met at the Olympics. I had not expected to hear from him again so soon.' *Sandi Jones*

They met up a number of times after this.
'He's absolutely great and we get on fabulously.' *Sandi Jones*

'There sometimes wasn't much romancing under the eye of Andrew's bodyguards, though we managed to give them the slip on occasions. Andrew can be extremely resourceful. He's just an ordinary guy who wants to have a fun time with his girlfriend.' *Sandi Jones*

Back at Gordonstoun Andrew regularly invited girls to stay with him during the holidays. Because of his good looks and Randy Andy image it was occasionally found necessary to squash the rumours of romance that were appearing in the press.
'He brings friends home with him every holiday. Naturally, like any other boy of his age he wants his family to meet them.' *Buckingham Palace spokesman*

'My only vice is women.' *Prince Andrew*

While still at Gordonstoun Andrew took a course at Number 1 Parachute Training School. He was interviewed after his first jump.

'Of course I was nervous. If you're not nervous you do something stupid. But I'm dead keen to do it again. Para-chuting is an experience I would never have wanted to miss.' *Prince Andrew*

He passed out of Dartmouth in April 1980, after which he was sent to the United States to join the commando ship Hermes *in Florida. Around this time he was interviewed about his love life.*
Prince Andrew: 'I don't believe I've ever been in love.'
Fellow midshipman: 'Except, of course, with yourself.'

Andrew had the aggravation of being followed all the time, either by his security man or the press.
'The security thing is becoming a bit of a bore. My detective's an excellent fellow, but it's a little uncomfortable to be accompanied everywhere. I sometimes feel like a public monument.' *Prince Andrew*

Of Prince Charles's visit to India in 1980: 'He'll probably drag along a lot of those newspaper chaps and perhaps I'll get a bit of peace.' *Prince Andrew*

After completing his elementary flying training, Andrew moved on to the Royal Naval air station at Culdrose in Cornwall to begin his training as a helicopter pilot. He spent part of his 21st birthday on 19 February 1981 up in a helicopter undergoing instruction. After the eighteen-week course he was awarded his wings, and won the silver salver for the midshipman with the highest marks. His father, as Admiral of the Fleet made the presentation.
'Congratulations, good luck and happy landings.' *Prince Philip*

When Andrew had qualified as a helicopter pilot he was promoted to the rank of sub-lieutenant and was posted to No 820 Squadron operating from the flight deck of the HMS Invincible. *He was very happy with his choice of career.*
'When I'm at sea I feel about six inches taller.' *Prince Andrew*

In 1978 he was measured at school.
'Guess what – I'm a whole bloody inch taller than my brother. It's the happiest day of my life.' *Prince Andrew*

Andrew did not become Guardian (head boy) like his father and elder brother in his last year at Gordonstoun, though he did become cricket captain. When Andrew finished at Gordonstoun he had gained six 'O' levels and three 'A' levels (in History, English, and Economics and Political Studies), but he had decided against continuing at university. He had already said that he wanted to pursue a career in the services as a naval pilot. In September 1979 he started at Britannia Royal Naval College in Dartmouth.

'You can ignore all that is going on in the rest of the world and get on with one's job.' *Prince Andrew*

Shortly after Andrew joined the Invincible *Argentina invaded the Falkland Islands, and the* Invincible *set off to help recapture them. There was talk of Andrew being pulled out.*

'He is a serving officer and there is no question in [the Queen's] mind that he should not go.' *Official statement from Buckingham Palace*

'I wouldn't like to be there in that weather. I feel a bit sorry for Andrew being tossed about on the high seas. But at least he can get into his aircraft and get off the ship for a while.' *Prince Charles*

'When there was fear, I overcame it with the simple maxim that I must think positive.' *Prince Andrew*

'He has been involved in many operations. Neither operational requirements, nor indeed Prince Andrew himself, would tolerate his being singled out for special treatment.' *Buckingham Palace spokesman*

'When you are in your anti-flash gear and are told to hit the deck because the ship is under attack there is nothing worse. You can only lie there and wait and hope. It's a most lonely feeling.' *Prince Andrew*

When his helicopter was attacked:
'For the first ten minutes we really didn't know which way to turn and what to do. I knew where I was and I was fairly frightened . . . It really makes the hair stand up on the back of your neck. It is not much fun having one of those fellows pick you out as a target.' *Prince Andrew*

An Exocet destroyed the ship the Atlantic Conveyor, *and Andrew and his team hovered over it winching members of the crew to safety while enemy shells came close.*
'I saw it being struck by the missile and it was something I will never forget. It was horrific. At the same time I saw a 4.5 shell come quite close to us. I saw my ship *Invincible* fire her missiles. Normally I would say it was spectacular, but it was my most frightening moment of the war.' *Prince Andrew*

The Falklands were recaptured on 14 June 1982. The first thing Andrew did was ring his mother.
'She was quite surprised to hear my voice. Her first words were how proud she was of the armed forces and for me to pass on the message that it had been a marvellous operation.' *Prince Andrew*

'It simply never occurred to me that because I'm a member of the Royal Family I wouldn't take part if it came to fighting and seeing it through. I was jolly glad that I was here throughout with my squadron.' *Prince Andrew*

Andrew stayed on in the Falklands until August, returning to Portsmouth on 17 September. He was away when Prince William was born.

On going home to England:
'I'm not looking forward to going back to being a Prince.' *Prince Andrew*

Once home, Andrew took a well-deserved holiday on the island of Mustique with girlfriend Koo Stark, a model/actress who was two years older than him. The media interest in the relationship was intense.
'Andrew came back from his holiday more drawn, more tired than he had from three months of war. He had every right to go on holiday. He wanted to get away from everything and unwind. Not only was he hounded over the affair, but hounded so much that he had to stop his holiday. I think that to treat someone who has gone out to serve their country like that is absolutely despicable. It really horrified me.' *Prince Edward*

In spite of the ferocious media attention, the Queen invited Koo to stay at Balmoral.
'She seems like a very nice girl.' *The Queen*

But eventually their relationship petered out. Andrew was awarded the South Atlantic Medal for his service in the Falklands.
'I feel different, but whether I sound, look or am different is for anyone to find out . . . I live to fly. I am a recluse. I try to keep out of people's way.' *Prince Andrew*

Asked what he wanted his future wife to be like:
'The honest answer is that I don't know what I'm looking for yet, simply because I haven't had any chance to think about it.' *Prince Andrew*

'I know that if I do find somebody, then it is going to come like a lightning bolt and you're going to know it there and then.' *Prince Andrew*

THE DUCHESS OF YORK

Sarah Margaret Ferguson was born on 15 October 1959 in London. Her father, Major Ronald Ferguson, once commanded the Sovereign's Escort of the Household Cavalry, and was nicknamed 'The General'. Her mother Susan (née Wright) had married Ronald when she was a teenager, and had Jane, her first daughter, about two years after marrying, and Sarah two years after that.

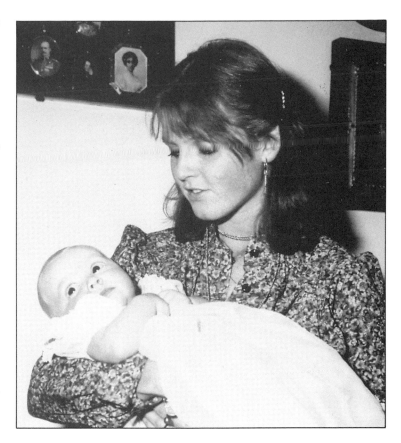

'A very good child, always cheerful and full of fun.' *Major Ronald Ferguson*

Sarah was brought up at Dummer Down Farm, near Basingstoke, Hampshire. She and her sister were well known for the way they would:
'Talk to the cowman and ploughman in the same polite way as they would to members of their own family.' *Chairman of the parish council*

Sarah started riding when she was three and was very good at it. At the age of five she was sent to Daneshill Prep School, Basingstoke, after which she attended Hurst Lodge, Sunningdale in Berkshire. She was a popular girl, but didn't think much of her marriage prospects.
'I don't think I'll ever get married. I can't imagine anyone wanting me.' *Sarah Ferguson*

In 1973 when Sarah was thirteen her mother left her father for Hector Barrantes, an Argentinian professional polo player.
'A bit of a fright, to put it mildly, for everyone.' *Major Ronald Ferguson*

Susan left without telling her daughters.
'I don't know how I told them that their mother had gone. I just know the feeling, knowing that she'd left me with two girls.' *Major Ronald Ferguson*

Sarah was a weekly boarder at the time, so her life went on much as usual. At home her father tried to make it up to both his daughters, but felt that his best wasn't good enough.
'It doesn't matter what the father is like or how much he takes upon himself, or what he does, there is no substitute whatever for a mother at that age.' *Major Ronald Ferguson*

'I hope the girls never realised how tough it was.' *Major Ronald Ferguson*

Sarah was moderately successful academically, and gained six 'O' levels and two CSEs. In her final year she was made head girl.

'We have so many girls coming and going that it is easy to forget them – but nobody ever forgot Sarah.' *One of her teachers*

When it was suggested that she took 'A' levels:
'What? 'A' levels? You must be joking!' *Sarah Ferguson*

Three years after Sarah's mother left, her father married again – another Susan. In time the second Mrs Ferguson had children of her own, Sarah's half-brother Andrew and two half-sisters, Alice and Eliza. After she left school Sarah did a course at Queen's Secretarial College. She had a number of jobs: working for a flat-letting agency, an art dealer and a sports PR agency. In 1984 she took a job with BCK, a graphic arts publishing company. Because it was small, her work was flexible, and she could do much of it from home. Apart from the money she earned, she received a small allowance from her father.

'When I say meagre, I mean meagre.' *Major Ronald Ferguson*

In June 1985 Sarah and her father were invited to stay at Windsor with the Queen and her family during Ascot Week, for the Guards Polo Club tournament. Prince Charles was playing, and Major Ferguson was his polo manager. Sarah had known Andrew vaguely before this, but there was no question of a romance. One of the main reasons she was invited was that she was a close friend of Diana, who would also be there.

Sarah's initial impression of Andrew:
'A big head who thinks a lot of himself.' *Sarah Ferguson*

'They met on the polo field – doesn't everybody?' *Susan Barrantes*

One night during that week Sarah was seated next to Andrew at dinner:
Sarah: 'He made me eat chocolate profiteroles, which I didn't want to eat at all.'
Andrew: 'I then didn't have any. So I got hit.'
Sarah: 'Very hard!'
Andrew: 'And it started from there.'

THE ENGAGEMENT

In January 1986 Sarah was invited to spend the New Year break with the Royal Family at Sandringham, and she and Andrew were glimpsed, possibly holding hands, by the press. The romance was then common property, and Sarah was followed everywhere. In early February Prince Charles and his family went to see Andrew on board his latest ship Brazen, and Sarah came along too, ostensibly as Diana's companion, and almost immediately afterwards the Prince and Princess of Wales went to Klosters for a skiing trip during which Sarah joined them. Shortly after this the engagement was announced.

'It has been quite an ordeal for a country girl. I am extremely proud of her. She has behaved absolutely perfectly, never holding her head down, always being polite, always smiling, yet never giving anything away.' *Major Ronald Ferguson*

'I think she's wonderful – but then I'm biased.' *Prince Charles*

'I think my brother is an exceedingly lucky man.' *Princess Anne*

The Princess of Wales to a group of photographers:
'You won't need me any more, now you've got Fergie!'

'He's met his match this time!' *The Queen*

'She's so *English*, so free of those airs and graces we can't stand.' *The Queen Mother*

The engaged couple were interviewed together after the engagement was announced. Asked whether marriage meant Andrew would be settling down:
'No, no. I mean, I don't see there's anything settling in it. It's a mighty upheaval for most people, and I think it'll be an upheaval for both of us.' *Prince Andrew*

Andrew: 'I think it's worth saying that I have no plans to change my Navy career, on the advice of Sarah.'
Sarah: 'Very strongly.'
Andrew: 'We discussed it at some length, and for the foreseeable future I will be continuing my naval career as it is at the moment. Sarah is quite prepared to put up with that, and I think she will be a remarkable wife if she can.'

'Biggles.' *Sarah's nickname for Andrew during the engagement*

'My job enables me to work from home, and I would be able to amalgamate my work with Andrew's career, and be a good wife to Andrew. I can cook too. You can do anything you want if you can put your mind to it . . . I think it's a case of where there's a will there's a way. I want to make sure I do things properly.' *Sarah Ferguson*

How she was going to learn to become Royal:
'Andrew has been a great help to me, and also the Queen, who has been at the end of a barrage of questions. She has been very long-suffering . . . But really it comes down to using your initiative and common sense.' *Sarah Ferguson*

On the day after the engagement was announced Sarah went to work as usual.
'I'm not going to change, why should I?' *Sarah Ferguson*

'I've got to get used to this "we" business.' *Prince Andrew*

Describing Andrew's best qualities:
'Wit, charm and good looks.' *Sarah Ferguson*

'We are a good team.' *Sarah Ferguson*

Why she was going to promise to "obey" at the wedding:
Sarah Ferguson: 'I was thinking of obeying in moral terms, as opposed to physically obeying. I am not the sort of woman who is going to meekly trot along behind. When I want to, I will stress a point. When we are in a dilemma or situation which needs someone to make a decision it will be Andrew who will take the lead. He will make the decision because he is the man of the marriage. Therefore in that sense I will obey him at one stage or another.'
Prince Andrew: 'But I promise to worship!'
Asked why they had chosen Westminster Abbey for the wedding:
Andrew: 'We could not really get married in Dummer Church, in Sarah's home village. We would not have been able to fit everyone in!'
Sarah: 'Andrew and I would quite happily get married anywhere, because we are marrying ourselves – and not the world.'

Asked how she would feel on her wedding day:
'I will be completely and utterly overexcited at the prospect of marrying the man waiting at the top of the aisle.' *Sarah Ferguson*

'It's going to be the best day of my life and that's all there is about it.' *Sarah Ferguson*

How would Andrew feel?
'I have no idea! But I will shout the answer to you across the Abbey if you want!' *Prince Andrew*

On how she was going to handle her new role:
'I'll just have to think slightly more, but I will not change when I go out. I'm just going to be me.' *Sarah Ferguson*

Diana's advice to Sarah on joining the Family Firm:
'Be delightful but discreet.' *The Princess of Wales*

Her father's advice:
'Be charming, co-operative, but say nothing.' *Major Ronald Ferguson*

THE MARRIAGE

Shortly before the wedding day it was announced that Andrew was to be made the Duke of York, a title last held by his grandfather George VI. It also meant that Sarah would be known as the Duchess of York, rather than Princess Andrew. They were married on 23 July 1986 in Westminster Abbey.

Sarah had been very involved with the planning; she specified:
'Lots of roses – and more flowers than at any other Royal wedding.' *Sarah Ferguson*

'I want it to be like something out of Cinderella.' *Sarah Ferguson*

As she was about to walk down the aisle with her father:
'Do you know the way?' *Sarah Ferguson*

On the balcony at Buckingham Palace afterwards:
Crowd: 'Kiss her! Kiss her!'
Andrew and Sarah (pretending): 'What? We can't hear you!'

Sarah had thoroughly enjoyed her wedding day, laughing, waving – and winking.
'She devalues the currency. All that winking at the wedding.' *Princess Michael of Kent*

'I don't see any reason why they shouldn't remain a marvellous pair. They are fun and they go about things in their own way. They're impromptu and outgoing, which shows in practically everything they do . . . Long may it last.' *Major Ronald Ferguson*

To her friends, after her marriage:
'Look you lot, it's Fergie or Sarah, none of this Your Highness nonsense, OK?' *The Duchess of York*

As they had agreed, Andrew remained in the Navy, which meant they spent much of the time apart.
'When Andrew is away I can't wait to see him – it's lonely being a Navy wife – especially when you're newly-wed.' *The Duchess of York*

'Andrew comes home on Friday absolutely tired out. On Saturday we have a row. On Sunday we make it up but by then he has got to go back to base again.' *The Duchess of York*

Sarah decided to learn to fly for Andrew's sake.
'Flying is his life and I want to be part of his life.' *The Duchess of York*

'I want to be able to sit down at dinner and discuss what he's done in the day. It's important for me to know how to fly so I can do that.' *The Duchess of York*

Prince Philip approved of Sarah taking lessons.
'I feel very strongly that flying isn't a sort of black art which can only be done by devotees or daredevils.' *Prince Philip*

After she got her helicopter wings she took Andrew on a flight.
'He didn't need a sick bag.' *The Duchess of York*

'She never ceases to amaze me.' *Prince Andrew*

Sarah continued to live up to her boast that she was a hard-working girl.
'The more you do the more you can do, and I love being a wife, I love my official duties and I love publishing . . . and I love flying too. So I'll just keep on doing as much as I can. Keeps you young.' *The Duchess of York*

On the lavatories in Buckingham Palace:
'Very good old fashioned loos which actually work really well, though they are the old fashioned ones with pulling up . . . You don't flush, you just pull up and it opens underneath, and water comes down and it works really well.' *The Duchess of York*

When presented with a buffalo head during Sarah and Andrew's first official tour of Canada in July 1987:
'I'll call it Andrew and hang it on the door.' *The Duchess of York*

At a dinner in Hollywood in February 1988 during the Yorks' tour of California, Sarah made some controversial comments:
'At last I have the turn to talk . . . all these men around here . . .' *The Duchess of York*
There followed wolf whistles and a shout from the crowd 'we love you', to which the Duchess replied:
'I'll see *you* later.'

In March 1987 Andrew publicly corrected Sarah.

'Why do you keep embarrassing me and pointing it out in front of other people when I get things wrong? It's not very charitable. Why don't you wait until we are on our own? . . . Unlike some people I haven't been doing this for 27 years. I'm going to make mistakes and get things wrong. You might as well accept that and help me.' *The Duchess of York*

At the end of the tour they embarked on a ten-day canoeing trip.

'I don't think I can stand ten days of this.' *The Duchess of York*

Andrew speaking at the same dinner:
'About eighteen months ago I made what is probably the greatest and best decision of my life – I married the woman at the end of the table.' *Prince Andrew*

'She is also expecting in August although some people may not have noticed.' *Prince Andrew*

Alluding to her pregnancy:
'So we decided – that is, all three of us – this person in here too . . .' *The Duchess of York*

On being pregnant:
'I can't wait to get the whole thing over with.' *The Duchess of York*

While she was pregnant Sarah joined a skiing trip to Klosters, for which she was castigated in the press as it could endanger her unborn child.
'I'm 100 per cent fit and I always moderate my skiing to suit the conditions.' *The Duchess of York*

It was during this trip that the Royal party went off piste and Major Hugh Lindsay was killed in an avalanche. Sarah was not with the Royal party when it happened.
'Klosters was a nightmare. I wish I had taken the advice to stay at home. I can't believe I was lucky enough not to be skiing that afternoon.' *The Duchess of York*

When presented with a rosette for a winning breed of Shire horse, during the latter stage of her pregnancy:
'Who gets the rosette – me or the horse? I'm beginning to feel like a horse.' *The Duchess of York*

'Sarah is very good with children, but somehow we've never talked about

'Last year I learned to fly; this year I'm going to have a baby; I'm wondering what to do next year.' *The Duchess of York*

how many she'd like.' *Jane Meakim, Sarah's sister*

There was growing speculation as to exactly when the new royal baby would arrive.
'Babies come when they are ready; they don't come to order.' *The Queen*

On 8 August 1988 at 8.18 a.m. Princess Beatrice Elizabeth Mary was born at the Portland Hospital, London.
'It feels wonderful to be a father. My daughter is gorgeous, but I'm biased. She is very pretty.' *Prince Andrew*

Six weeks after the birth of Princess Beatrice, the Duchess of York went on a long tour of Australia, where she was reunited with Prince Andrew, who had been serving on board his ship.

Defending Sarah's decision to leave their daughter behind:
'Beatrice is much better off at home where things are stable.' *Prince Andrew*

Media criticism of Sarah's separation from Beatrice increased. But she didn't let it bother her.
'I wouldn't go to bed crying about it.' *The Duchess of York*

'I've been told that sailors' wives don't want children around when their husbands are on shore leave.' *The Duchess of York*

Sarah had been on a strict diet since the birth.
'I was determined to look pretty and thin when I saw Andrew again.' *The Duchess of York*

On the problems of their long-distance marriage:
'Before getting married I never bothered about going away because it was fun. But I think to be split from one's wife for so long cannot be good for the long-term relationship.' *Prince Andrew*

On how he kept up with his daughter's progress:
'Sarah has been very, very good taking photographs and sending them to me. She is also keeping a video of Beatrice and it will all be recorded for her in years to come and for me to see when I get back.' *Prince Andrew*

When asked if Beatrice was missing her while in Australia:
'She's not missing me, but I'm missing her.' *The Duchess of York*

When someone asked her if she wanted to hold their baby while on a walkabout:
'If I hug one, I'll be here all day.' *The Duchess of York*

When asked in July 1989 when she was planning to have another baby:
'I'm in no hurry to get pregnant.' *The Duchess of York*

'I've worked very hard to get my figure back and I'm enjoying the results. I don't want to give it all away too soon.' *The Duchess of York*

On 9 September 1989 the Duchess of York was one of the first guests on Sue Lawley's late night show Saturday Matters. *Sue asked her about a school report which once described Sarah as: 'Slapdash, stubborn and headstrong.'*
'I always tried to do things and not get caught. I put dye in the lavatory cistern, and put glue on the teacher's

chair – because it was maths – I didn't like maths.' *The Duchess of York*

When asked on the same programme what Princess Beatrice's reaction was to Sarah's 'Budgie' books:
'When I showed it to her, she did her normal trick, and tore it up and threw it in the dustbin.' *The Duchess of York*

On 12 September 1989 it was announced that Sarah was expecting a second baby. When asked whether she was hoping for a boy this time:
'I just want a happy, healthy baby and a friend for Beatrice. It will be nice for her to have someone to play with. I'm pleased there will not be a very great age gap between her and the new baby.' *The Duchess of York*

When asked if she was really pleased she replied:
'Of course. I'm more than pleased. I'm ecstatic.' *The Duchess of York*

On 23 March 1990 Sarah was admitted to the Portland Hospital and gave birth to a daughter by Caesarian section. A week later, when Sarah left the hospital, it was announced that the baby would be named Eugenie Victoria Helena and would be known officially as Her Royal Highness Princess Eugenie of York. Eugenie was the name of one of Queen Victoria's granddaughters, the daughter of Princess Beatrice.

─── PRINCESS BEATRICE ───

'She's got Andrew's lips.' *The Duchess of York*

'She's going to be a carrot-top just like me.' *The Duchess of York*

'It's only a tinge of hair so far, but it's quite clearly the same colour as my own.' *The Duchess of York*

'She has got Sarah's eyes and I am convinced she is going to be prettier than both of us.' *Prince Andrew*

'She's just incredibly placid and calm, sleeps through the night. I don't know where she gets it from, probably her father.' *The Duchess of York*

'I look around and I can't believe how lucky I am – a good husband and a good baby.' *The Duchess of York*

THE REAL PRINCE ANDREW

'The one with the Robert Redford looks.' *Prince Charles*

'He is my support, my main right arm.' *The Duchess of York*

When he wears a kilt:
'There's nothing worn under it. It's all in good working order.' *Prince Andrew*

'Many people have wanted to hit Andrew, but I'm the only one who's dared. And look where it's got me!' *The Duchess of York*

'Andrew is like a teddy bear – cuddly.' *The Duchess of York*

Looking round a girl's flat when a bachelor:
'So good to be in a normal home – it takes me ages to find the kitchen at the Palace.' *Prince Andrew*

On photography:
'My family always cringe when they hear the sound of a motor-drive, even if it is mine.' *Prince Andrew*

On his own photographs:
'I have noticed one or two of them that are interestingly strange. I didn't look at things this way before and I dare say the theme for some strange reason is loneliness. If you look at them as a package, there is not much there. There is nobody in them.' *Prince Andrew*

Meeting the actor Michael Caine:
'My brother knows lots of stars, but I don't.' *Prince Andrew*

Asked about medals:
'You should talk to my brother Charles, the Prince of Wales. He has a yard of medals and they don't mean a thing.' *Prince Andrew*

On spraying photographers with white paint:
'I enjoyed that!' *Prince Andrew*
Apologising later:
'It was a complete accident and very unfortunate. I think I probably learnt my lesson to point the paint in the right direction next time . . . towards the wall, which is in fact what I did, but by that time it was too late.' *Prince Andrew*

Why he likes clowning around:
'I become bored with being myself and like taking on other roles. My brother [Prince Charles] is far better at dramatics. I make a comedian of myself.' *Prince Andrew*

'He is the most incredible husband, he is the one who gets me through, he's always there, he's a rock.' *The Duchess of York*

To waiting photographers in Los Angeles sporting a Union Jack and Stars and Stripes in her hair:
'Check out the hair boys.' *The Duchess of York*

THE REAL
── DUCHESS OF YORK ──

'Sarah is vivacious, cheerful, outgoing, vibrant. She sparkles, radiating warmth and a sense of fun. There is another word I can use, but I'm not going to say it . . .' *Prince Andrew*

'I do have two sides. I have an extremely hard-working and thoughtful side too.' *The Duchess of York*

'Now she's a Duchess, but it can't change a person's way of being, especially someone like Sarah. My daughter will always be the same. She keeps on being authentic, a real person. She is fun and affectionate and yet she is determined and a real fighter.' *Susan Barrantes*

'Sarah's the family manager holding the purse-strings.' *Prince Andrew*

'She's a very open girl. She loves to make people feel happy.' *Prince Andrew*

When meeting a severely physically disabled person, who was unsure how to address her: 'Just call me Fergie.'

'I am a service wife first.' *The Duchess of York*

'I know about going for a job and an interview. I never had my own flat, always rented rooms and know all the pitfalls.' *The Duchess of York*

On fitness:
'Where there's a will there's a way, I find the will and then I find the way.' *The Duchess of York*

'I think the Royal Family like her a great deal, although I would not presume to say whether she has had a profound affect on them. That would suggest there was something wrong with them before she came along! That is, of course, not the case.' *Major Ronald Ferguson*

When his daughter was supposedly called 'common' and a 'Coronation Street Princess' by Princess Michael of Kent:
'*We* find it more dignified to remain silent.' *Major Ronald Ferguson*

'Behind every man there's a good woman? I mean an *exhausted* one.' *The Duchess of York*

As she worked in publishing, had she ever thought of writing a book herself?
'Yes, but I haven't totally and utterly taken it out of the computer between my ears . . . I do have very specific ideas but I'm afraid I'm not going to let you know. Is that all right? I don't mean to be rude.' *The Duchess of York*

On criticisms that she neglects her official duties:
'My immediate reaction is "if only they knew". I was called a parasite the other day by some student. It's so sad but it's not their fault. I really do care when someone shouts out "parasite", of course it's going to affect you, I am not inhuman, you know, but I don't pick up the papers and say "Boo hoo what am I going to do about it?" I just get on with the next thing.' *The Duchess of York*

'She was 26 when she got married, so she was already streetwise. It's terribly important to be streetwise in this modern age.' *Major Ronald Ferguson*

'I keep my head up, unlike some people I could mention.' *The Duchess of York*

On why she posed for photographers on her 1987 skiing trip.
'I've always had a good relationship with them and I intend to keep it that way . . . If I'm going to have my picture taken, I want to look as good as possible.' *The Duchess of York*

On accepting an inscribed catalogue of David Hockney's retrospective exhibition to mark his 50th birthday:
'There is no T in Duchess . . .' *The Duchess of York*

'There are 25 hours in a day. I've proved it! . . . I burn the candle at both ends and I get up far too early, which means . . . my weekends are spent asleep.' *The Duchess of York*

'The busier you are the more you get done. It's a tonic, it keeps me in touch with the world around me . . . The girls in the office insist I'm a workaholic which drives them mad. And I want to do it because at the end of the day when Andrew comes back I have actually been doing something, I haven't just been sitting there wondering what I'm going to put on the next day.' *The Duchess of York*

On how she kept alive her interest in publishing during her pregnancy and wrote two children's books, Budgie The Little Helicopter *and* Budgie At Bendick's Point, *which were published in 1989:*
'My husband was going to sea for six months. I was pregnant and I felt it was a good time to start.' *The Duchess of York*

'She is strong and independent. You watch Fergie change us all.' *Princess Michael of Kent*

'I want to look good. I don't want people to think I am grumpy. I want to look my best.' *The Duchess of York*

Why she prefers walking to riding these days:
'It's my legs which need the exercise, not the horse.' *The Duchess of York*

After a gruelling walkabout:
'My feet are killing me.' *The Duchess of York*

Her idea of how a woman should look:
'A trim waist, a good up-top and enough down the bottom but not too big . . . I'm quite happy with my figure, quite happy with myself.' *The Duchess of York*

'You can be so hidebound by fashion that you end up tying yourself in knots . . . dress the way you want to dress.' *Prince Andrew*

SARAH AND APPEARANCE

'Cream cakes, no, I don't see eye to eye . . . I'm savoury, I'm sausages.' *The Duchess of York*

Why she does not cook:
'Because if I did I would eat too much and put on more weight.' *The Duchess of York*

About life in Buckingham Palace:
'It certainly encourages me to lose weight. There is never any food there and if I have to order it, I have to think about it.' *The Duchess of York*

'Naturally she got quite upset at various stages about the criticism – her weight and all that – but as I explained to her, unfortunately, she's no longer a private person. She's a public person now . . . She went into it with her eyes wide open.' *Major Ronald Ferguson*

'I'm just going to be me. To begin with I made the dreadful mistake of taking in what the fashion people wrote . . . but I don't really want to change. I'm quite happy with myself.' *The Duchess of York*

7

PRINCE EDWARD

Prince Edward was born on 10 March 1964, the fourth child and third son of the Queen and Prince Philip. Charles and Anne, who were both away at school when he was born, were given time off to come and see their new brother. It was to be a bumper year for royal births: within a few months Princess Margaret also gave birth to Lady Sarah, Princess Alexandra to James and the Duchess of Kent to Lady Helen.

'When the fourth child comes along, in most cases it's unintentional.' *Prince Philip*

The baby prince was christened Edward Antony Richard Louis on 2 May in the private chapel of Windsor Castle.
'The quietest of my children.' *The Queen*

After taking Edward to his first classical concert:
'I have never known a child to sit so still.' *The Queen Mother*

Like his elder brothers and sister, Edward first started 'school' at Buckingham Palace. His governess was Miss Lavinia Keppel, and he shared his class with five other pupils, including Lady Sarah Armstrong-Jones and

James Ogilvy. At the age of seven Edward became a day-boy at Gibbs, a preparatory school in Kensington, and James Ogilvy again accompanied him. Finally he followed his two elder brothers to Gordonstoun.
'I don't think Gordonstoun's as tough as it used to be, but it's certainly an outdoor school and when you've been living in Scotland for most of the year for five years you get used to a colder climate.' *Prince Edward*

'I don't agree with the statement that schooldays are the happiest days of your life. Although I will admit that my last term at Gordonstoun was probably the most enjoyable.' *Prince Edward*

'Jaws.' *Prince Edward's nickname at Gordonstoun when he wore braces on his teeth*

'Earl.' *Prince Edward's other nickname, taken from his initials*

'Edward Bishop.' *The name Prince Edward travelled under in 1977 on a school trip to Italy*

In 1982 Edward went to New Zealand for two terms to teach as a junior master at Wanganui School. This is how he introduced himself on the first morning:
'Good morning, I'm afraid you know a great deal more about me than I do about you. I'm hopeless with names. You'll have to be patient.' *Prince Edward*

Asked whether he dated any girls during that time:
'It would be pointless to say no. People are going to say "What's wrong with him?" I haven't been to many dances. Just one. Mostly I have been out to dinner with members of the school staff.' *Prince Edward*

General impressions of New Zealand:
'What I like about New Zealand is the friendliness. It hit me when I first came here. It may be partly because people emigrated here and it was sparsely populated and they always wanted to know their neighbours. It's probably a hangover from that and makes life better.' *Prince Edward*

Shopping for himself in New Zealand:
'I've been down to town several times to stock up the larder. I was in a supermarket and there were a few embarrassing moments with people not paying attention where they pushed their trolleys. One housewife was absolutely amazed that I should be there in the first place and failed to accept that it's just down the road and very convenient.' *Prince Edward*

'The thing I've missed most is family and friends, obviously. There's no particularly British institutions that I miss as this is a very British society.' *Prince Edward*

After his return Edward became an undergraduate at Cambridge.
'I have a whole lot of friends at Cambridge, but you can't be exclusive, it's as simple as that. The media can make what they like of anything. You only have to be seen in the company of one person more than three times and you arc instantly virtually married to them.' *Prince Edward*

'These have been three of the best years of my life that I am likely to spend . . . There's a wonderful mix of people and I am never likely to mix so informally with such a wide range of people.' *Prince Edward*

At Cambridge Edward became involved with acting, as Charles had done.
'It initially helped me overcome shyness and gave me the ability to stand up in front of people, which is a very useful training and education.' *Prince Edward*

'I certainly didn't get a very good degree, it was pretty mediocre. I found revision incredibly tedious. I hope that in the three years I have been here I have done other things.' *Prince Edward*

Edward had long ago decided to make his career with the Marines, which he joined after Cambridge.
'The Marines are looking forward to having me if only to rub my nose in it. Everybody thinks I'm mad. It's probably the greatest challenge I will ever have to meet.' *Prince Edward*

But Edward had not been long in the Marines when it was announced that he was leaving.
'It was a very agonising decision. Four years ago I wanted to be a Marine. But having got here I changed my mind and decided that the services generally – not just the Royal Marines

– was not the career I wanted.' *Prince Edward*

On what he planned to do next:
'Heaven knows.' *Prince Philip*

'The difficulty is finding a job that will not cause an inordinate amount of pressure on the people I work for or with. It requires a considerable amount of tact and I am not a free agent.' *Prince Edward*

There followed a year of uncertainty about his career which Edward later described as: 'The worst year of my life.'

While looking around for a job Edward decided to orchestrate a version of It's A Knockout *and persuaded other members of the Royal Family to join him as participants, the proceeds going to charity.*
'It's an experiment, a very radical venture.' *Prince Edward*

'A joust the like of which you have never seen before and never will again.' *Prince Edward*

How he was 'persuaded' to take an active role in the venture:
'We got everybody together and explained the game plan. Then I was going to do my usual thing, which was to sit back and let them get on with it. And that's when they all turned around and said "Not on your life".' *Prince Edward*

'I would like the public to view it in a generous way – seeing that members of the Royal Family are, in reality, ordinary human beings. We're not superstars. And I hope, at the end of the competition, the Royal Family will come out of it much better.' *Prince Edward*

'I have decided I wish to be other than a member of an elite, any elite – I'm not a Rambo.' *Prince Edward*

'I could enjoy a life in the theatre very much indeed.' *Prince Edward*

Although the final programme was judged to have been in poor taste, it raised over a million pounds for charity.

'It was an experiment and a lot of people have learnt from it. I seem to have lost everything and gained very little.' *Prince Edward*

'I've learned a lot from "Knock-Out"; it has to be said that, having got so much involved in it, I've actually got my hands dirty; and that sort of hands-on experience is never forgotten. But hopefully I'll find something less in the forefront.' *Prince Edward*

On what he intended to do next:
'I have a lot of plans going.' *Prince Edward*

In January 1988 it was announced that Edward would join Andrew Lloyd Webber's Really Useful Theatre Company as a production assistant.
'I am delighted with the prospect of joining the company to learn more about the theatre professionally.' *Prince Edward*

'I am delighted that Prince Edward is going to join the staff. I have been impressed by his real enthusiasm for the theatre and genuine desire to learn the business.' *Andrew Lloyd Webber*

A former production assistant describing the job:
'A really mixed bag. You do a little of everything. . . . you're a real dogsbody.'

A year later, Edward had won the admiration of the Really Useful staff.
'He has become part of our team. If anything needs doing with any of our productions, Edward is there to muck in.' *Director*

THE REAL PRINCE EDWARD

'I may be a human being but I certainly wouldn't describe myself as normal. And that can never be the case. I mean if you have ever followed me down the street you notice people turn and always do a double take – and then again I am always accompanied by a policeman.' *Prince Edward*

'I've looked after myself. I have cooked for myself. I am incredibly modest – but I'll tell you I am an excellent cook.' *Prince Edward*

On being a Prince (while at Cambridge):
'I actually enjoy being what I am. Basically because I have just got used to it and at this moment in time I am having a really good time of it. It has its ups and downs, but everything has its ups and downs.' *Prince Edward*

The down side of being a Prince:
'It must be the quickest way of losing friends. They are caught up in all the attention I get.' *Prince Edward*

'The material side of things is not really important in this job at all. You've got to try to keep up some sort of appearance.' *Prince Edward*

Why his time as an undergraduate was important:
'Very much being my own boss and running my life the way I wanted to do it – which is probably something off the beaten track as far as many are concerned.' *Prince Edward*

'I have obviously had a few pitfalls along the way and made mistakes, but then again if one does make mistakes there is still someone to pick you up.' *Prince Edward*

On acting:
'I can get quite absorbed in the character I am playing on stage. The stage is a wonderful world of fantasy and make-believe where actors can help people forget the troubles and cares of the world to escape for a little.' *Prince Edward*

'Mr Shakespeare.' *The name Prince Edward travelled under on a flight for Scotland*

EDWARD ON THE PRESS

'There's a difference between a public function when you know the press will be there and a private one where, to me, their presence is an invasion of privacy. I don't mind a photograph being taken on the lawn.' *Prince Edward*

When besieged by paparazzi during the celebratory dinner after the opening night of the Lloyd-Webber musical Aspects Of Love:
'You know the rules, now bugger off.' *Prince Edward*

Shown a picture of himself taking photos of press photographers taking pictures of him:
'I rather liked that. I abide by the saying "If you can't beat 'em, join 'em."' *Prince Edward*

Edward was given a bad press for his decision to leave the Marines.
'Inevitably that was nasty because

they were never going to understand and there was no way I was going to take the time to explain it to them. It wouldn't have worked because they would still write what they wanted.'
Prince Edward

When his name was linked romantically with that of millionaire's daughter, Georgie May:
'I don't know what you're talking about. It's all complete fabrication.'
Prince Edward

EDWARD ON THE HOMELESS

On the plight of young destitutes:
'They are prey to pimps and pushers. By accident, I am sure, their plight is about to get worse. For thanks to the reorganization of the welfare benefits – a much needed effort in the long term – one or two anomalies have appeared, one of which is the ending of any sort of benefits to sixteen and seventeen-year-olds. This blow is only one of the many which can wreck a young life. For once in the homeless trap it is merely a vicious downward spiral with no escape.' *Prince Edward*

'Nobody becomes homeless by choice – so utterly broke they are reduced to begging. Nobody.' *Prince Edward*

'Don't ask me why, but most adults are embarrassed to admit they were ever a teenager, let alone that they may have made mistakes. Most people switch off when they hear such things. Most people were unconcerned about drug abuse until AIDS came along.'
Prince Edward

On meeting his waxworks dummy in Madame Tussauds:
'Hmm . . . he's got more hair. That's slightly embarrassing.' *Prince Edward*

On being Royal:
'There's a certain amount of acting involved. If you played the part of a member of the Royal Family as a down-to-earth character it probably wouldn't work.' *Prince Edward*

8

THE ROYAL COUSINS

THE DUKE AND DUCHESS OF GLOUCESTER

Prince Richard, the Duke of Gloucester, was born on 26 August 1944, the second son of the then Duke and Duchess, Henry and Alice. He married Birgitte Von Deurs in July 1972, and only one month later his elder brother William, heir to the Dukedom, was killed in a plane crash. His father had suffered a bad stroke in June 1968 and died in 1974, making Richard the new Duke. He had studied as an architect, and until his brother's death had no intention of taking on any Royal duties. They have three children: Alexander, the Earl of Ulster, born in 1974; Lady Davina Windsor, born in 1977; and Lady Rose Windsor, born in 1980.

On his childhood:
'The highlights were the summer holidays in Scotland, I always looked forward to going home ... I enjoyed my life at Cambridge because for the first time I had freedom ... William said that the people who taught History were rather dull. He was under the mistaken impression that I was good at drawing, so he suggested I try Architecture.' *The Duke of Gloucester*

Asked, as an architect, if the Elgin marbles should be returned to Athens:
'No. It would be more sensible to ship the rest of the Parthenon here.' *The Duke of Gloucester*

On having to give up architecture after his father died:

'I suppose I would have been very depressed if it hadn't been for the fact that I inherited the farm with my title. I think if it hadn't been for the farm, I'd have been rather roofless.' *The Duke of Gloucester*

About belonging to the Royal Family:

'The funny thing with the Royal Family is that as you grow older you become less senior . . . I quite like the idea of it not being a full-time job.' *The Duke of Gloucester*

About his book of photographs on Oxford and Cambridge:

'Doing books is a very good discipline . . . You set out as though you were on a hunting trip, you stalk what you are after and come back quite exhausted.' *The Duke of Gloucester*

'I often wonder if the Nazis had invaded Britain would I have become a guerilla, a collaborator or just taken up knitting and pretended it wasn't happening.' *The Duke of Gloucester*

'I would love to see Gaddafi in his swimming trunks because I suspect with his large head and triangular shape he must pad his shoulders immensely. I suspect he has a very small body.' *The Duke of Gloucester*

About the Duke and Duchess of Gloucester:

'They work as hard as we ever did, and incomparably harder than we did before the war. But they cannot afford a chauffeur, a lady's maid or a valet. We have to share such help as best we can and for much of his day's business the Duke dodges about London on his motorbike.' *Princess Alice, the Duke's mother*

Lamenting the fact that his wife would be known as Duchess rather than Princess: 'Being a Duchess sounds like someone old and haughty, whereas one thinks of a Princess as being young and beautiful.' *The Duke of Gloucester*

THE DUKE AND DUCHESS OF KENT

Prince Edward George Nicholas Paul Patrick, eldest son of Prince George, Duke of Kent and Princess Marina, was born on 10 October 1935. A few hours before he was born a strange black cat walked up to the house and sat outside the front door until after his birth. He became Duke of Kent at the age of six when his father died. Eddie went to Eton and then to Sandhurst. As a young man he was a bit of a tearaway, who liked fast cars – and wrote off two of them. In 1956 when he was 21 he was posted to Catterick camp, where he met the 23-year-old Katherine Worsley. He fell very much in love with her, but his mother was against the match initially. They were not allowed to become engaged until 1961, six years after they first met, which included a whole year when they weren't allowed to meet. They were married on 8 June 1961 at York Minster: Katherine was determined *not* to be married at Westminster Abbey. Their three children are George the Earl of St Andrews, who was born in 1962, Lady Helen Windsor, who was born in 1964 and Lord Nicholas Windsor, who was born in 1970. In 1976 the Duchess of Kent miscarried her fourth child in the fifth month of pregnancy, after which she suffered on and off from depression for the next eight years – so severely in 1979 that she was hospitalised for six weeks. The Duke of Kent had to sell the family home of Coppins in 1974, and in 1976 he left the army to become the vice-chairman of the British Overseas Trade Board.

'No matter how monarchy changes – and change it must – Charles will need the support of people like Eddie and Alexandra. They don't grow on trees, you know. To be a monarch and have cousins like the Kents is of untold value – they are both relatives, friends and, at the same time, bloody hard-working people.' *Lord Mountbatten*

About her marriage in 1983:
'We are the luckiest people in the world.' *The Duchess of Kent*

Before opening Helen House, a hospice for dying children, in 1983:
'I've been to so many hospices, but this is my first children's one and it is *so* important. I don't really know how it will affect me, I'm not very robust.' *The Duchess of Kent*

About her frequent visits to Helen House:
'I feel privileged and humble, drained sometimes, terribly drained because you give an awful lot. I have never felt sad. After I had been here four or five times it suddenly dawned on me how tears and smiles walk side by side.' *The Duchess of Kent*

'People often ask me why these children mean so much to me. Why do I love them so much. Yet they're so loving. Sometimes I find it very hard to believe that these beautiful children will be returning to God at such a tender age. If people say that their eyes light up when I'm with them, they should look into mine. They light up, too.' *The Duchess of Kent*

'I do think that I helped to make the Kents the people they are today. I taught them to shake hands faster than anyone else – at least, when pushed, twenty people a minute!' *Lord Mountbatten*

To a little girl who asked her the question:
'No darling, I don't live with the Queen – I would get in her way because she's very busy.' *The Duchess of Kent*

Asked by a little girl, 'What do you do with all those heavenly grapes?'
'I couldn't think what she meant. Then the child said that in the prayer book the prayer for the Royal Family says, "Enrich them with your heavenly grapes." I didn't tell her it wasn't grapes, it was Grace. Instead I thought about the most marvellous days we could have on Sundays – eating those lovely grapes!' *The Duchess of Kent*

'Fortunately I am never going to have to carry out official engagements like my parents. I have managed to remain anonymous so far in life and I want to stay that way.' *The Earl of St Andrews*

On starting work at Christie's Auctioneers in 1984:
'It is my first serious job. And I want to make my career working in contemporary art . . . It's very hard work, but really interesting.' *Lady Helen Windsor*

'I want to have a serious career . . . I always appear in such a frivolous light in the newspapers.' *Lady Helen Windsor*

About her nickname 'Melons':
'I hate my nickname! Of course I object to it. I don't know where it came from in the first place. Everyone who knows me calls me Helen – and that's the way I like it. Melons is just plain silly.' *Lady Helen Windsor*

PRINCESS ALEXANDRA
——AND ANGUS OGILVY——

Princess Alexandra, the Queen's cousin and one of the most popular members of the Royal Family, was born on Christmas Day 1936, the daughter of Prince George, the Duke of Kent, and Princess Marina. She was christened Alexandra Helen Elizabeth Olga, and her grandmother Queen Mary, who had witnessed the death of her husband and the abdication of her eldest son during 1936, said that her birth was 'the only nice thing to have happened this year'. She was the first Princess to go to school – Heathfield – which she left when she was sixteen. Alexandra first met Angus Ogilvy in

'I am indeed overwhelmed with pride about Alexandra possessing the wonderful gift of spreading happiness around her.' *Princess Marina*

1953, but they didn't start dating until 1956. He was a businessman eight years her senior, who although not Royal himself had always moved in Royal circles. He was educated at Eton, then spent time with the Scots Guards before going to Trinity College Oxford. He started to work in the City after a brief period in the Merchant Navy. They were married in June 1963, and Alexandra was the first Royal to have a wedding present list – which she lodged at Harrods. In 1969

Ogilvy was linked with a City scandal, and because of his Royal connections he had to resign all his directorships. His income fell from £90,000 to £9,000 overnight. After this he was able to accompany his wife more on Royal duties, and he was also invited to become financial adviser to Sotheby's. They have two children, James Ogilvy, who was born in 1964, and Marina Ogilvy who was born in 1966.

'She is the most marvellous person. I do not think I can honestly fault her in anything. To me she epitomises all that is best in the family.' *Prince William of Gloucester*

Why she refused to press a button which started a computer:
'I just didn't like the way the man asked me to do it. I thought, I won't do it. Why should I?' *Princess Alexandra*

When someone wanted to write a biography of her:
'I could understand it if I was a great actress like Bernhardt, or a scientist like Marie Curie; then there would be something to write about. But I've done nothing. Why, only yesterday I opened a turbine mill.' *Princess Alexandra*

On the Royal Family's general popularity:
'Don't forget that nowadays we have to compete with Elizabeth Taylor and the Beatles.' *Princess Alexandra*

Of her son, who was born on 29 February:
'It was bad enough for me, sharing a birthday on Christmas Day. I didn't want my poor child only to have birthdays every four years.' *Princess Alexandra*

'I don't see why I should get a peerage just because I've married a Princess.' *Angus Ogilvy*

Caught smoking in Australia, despite being president of the Imperial Cancer Fund:
'It was the flies. I lit a cigarette to get rid of them. And of course that was that. But I've vowed to stop the moment I get back to London.' *Angus Ogilvy*

On the same visit to Australia:
'I almost got arrested for being too near my own wife!' *Angus Ogilvy*

'My wife is very good at talking to people – she's been trained to it since childhood – but she's also genuinely interested in people. I'm afraid I'm no good at it. I sometimes think it would be much easier if we went back to the old days when you didn't speak to Royalty until they spoke to you. Then we wouldn't have to say anything – much easier.' *Angus Ogilvy*

'I was a little beast sometimes, so I'll make sure my children aren't spoilt.' *Princess Alexandra*

'You decide to spend an evening with the children, but then someone rings up and says, "Will you please come to a film première? If you come it will help us raise another £1,500 and this could help 300 spastics." Well, who are more important?' *Angus Ogilvy*

'We are trying to bring up two children with their feet firmly on the ground. When they grow up they will each have to earn their own livings. Being related to the Queen will not help them and nor will the fact that they spend holidays in magnificent castles assist them to get on in life.' *Angus Ogilvy*

'I decided we wouldn't release pictures of me for my eighteenth birthday. The last official ones were taken when I was about twelve. I thought that while I was working, life would be much easier if people didn't recognise me.' *Marina Ogilvy*

In 1986 Marina joined Operation Raleigh, an adventure scheme for young people, in the Honduras.
Why she wanted to go:
'I felt very trapped and low. A year before, I had had peritonitis and was anorexic for a time. I had become very withdrawn, and though both my parents were very supportive I think they worried about me. I'm not a rebel, but I felt I wanted to make my own friends rather than be pushed into being an upper-class sort of girl. You don't make friends by going to a succession of parties or by getting drunk or being stupid, you make friends *doing* things.' *Marina Ogilvy*

'I honestly thought the interviewers would turn me down if they knew about Mum. They might think I was trying to get in on my name.' *Marina Ogilvy*

'When I finally got accepted I was so excited I rang up Prince Charles in tears.' *Marina Ogilvy*

How she liked it:
'The main thing is I feel accepted. I've made friends with people I'd never meet otherwise. I can't tell you how much it means to me to have someone come up and give me a great big hug.' *Marina Ogilvy*

'One thing I've learned. If you want to cry – cry. You shouldn't be embarrassed about anything, whether it's stripping off all your clothes or being ribbed about the family. Clothes and make-up don't matter.' *Marina Ogilvy*

'I hope all this will help Operation Raleigh and will also change some people's views of the "Young Royals". Personally I don't like the image of racy, upper-class little kids bumming around. I find their lives selfish and false. They have never *done* anything or experienced anything worthwhile.' *Marina Ogilvy*

On the morning of 9 October 1989 the British public awoke to sensational press reports that Marina was expecting a baby – out of wedlock. The father-to-be was named as her boyfriend of two years, freelance photographer Paul Mowatt. In a six-page interview in the tabloid press an amazing public row unfolded as she claimed her parents had given her an 'abortion or shotgun marriage' *ultimatum:* 'Dad said there hadn't been an illegitimate birth in the Royal Family for 150 years. When I said to him "Look, I am your daughter, won't you help me. What comes first, Queen and country or your own daughter," he said: "Queen and country".' *Marina Ogilvy*

Marina claimed that following her refusal to take either option offered, her parents had cut her off without a penny: 'My mother is a total hypocrite. When it counted, she wasn't there for me . . . This is the dark side of the Royal Family. The other side of the postcard is for the tourists.' *Marina Ogilvy*

'My father loves being married to a Royal. He has always gloried in it. It's a bit weird really.' *Marina Ogilvy*

The family were reconciled in time for the wedding on 2 February 1990.

'There have been a lot of misunder-
standings with my parents, but I think
it was just basically growing up.'
Marina Ogilvy

PRINCE AND PRINCESS
─── MICHAEL OF KENT ───

Prince Michael of Kent was born on 4 July 1942 and christened Michael George Charles Franklin. He was only seven weeks old when his father Prince George, Duke of Kent, died in an air crash. Like his elder brother he loved dangerous sports and once narrowly missed breaking his neck. In 1972 he met Marie Christine, then married to his friend Tom Troubridge. Marie Christine was born on 15 January 1945 in Czechoslovakia, shortly after which her parents moved to Vienna. Her parents were divorced in 1950. Her father remarried and became a wild game hunter, while she moved with her mother and brother to Australia. She married Troubridge in 1971. They divorced in 1977, after having been separated for three years. The marriage was annulled in 1978 on the grounds that her husband would not give her children. She married Prince Michael – and became Princess Michael – on 30 July 1978 in Vienna Town Hall. Because Marie Christine was a Catholic, Prince Michael had to renounce his right to the throne when he married her. In 1980 Prince Michael took a job in the City. They have two children (who are being brought up as Protestants): Lord Frederick Windsor, born 6 April 1979 and Lady Gabriella Windsor, born 23 April 1980.

On his reckless driving:
'If his driver's driving he'll be here in three hours. If he's driving, in two.' *Princess Michael*

'I believe that every man has a special place in his heart for one woman above all others and also for one car.' *Prince Michael*

On failing his first driving test:
'I arrived to take the test wearing a yellow carnation in my buttonhole which put off the examiner, who thought it rather distasteful.' *Prince Michael*

'I am the one who appears strong, but he is my rock, he never fails me.' *Princess Michael*

On his first meeting with Marie Christine:
'I was very struck by this tall Austrian lady. I was very impressed. I remember we had a long talk about the history of art sitting in a hut eating sausages.' *Prince Michael*

Her first impression of him:
'I just thought he was the funniest man I had ever met. We just kept laughing and talking together. But I didn't think he really "noticed" me at all. He was with such a pretty girl.' *Princess Michael*

'I was unsuitable, quite unsuitable, as a Royal bride. I am Catholic and I was also the first tall woman to marry into the Royal Family.' *Princess Michael*

'Marriage is finding someone you can share a flat with.' *Princess Michael*

About her husband leaving the army for the City:
'We were trying to earn our living respectably by my husband getting work. But he couldn't advertise "PRINCE – AVAILABLE FOR DIRECTORSHIPS". He couldn't be head-hunted. So how were people to know that, except by spreading the word as you do at dinner parties or when you meet important people and say, "Oh, by the way, my husband's now out of the army and he's looking for work in the City." ' *Princess Michael*

On press attention:
'We didn't realise that we would be so public. My husband never had been, so we didn't think anybody would find us all that interesting.' *Princess Michael*

Memories of their wedding ball in Vienna:
'Michael and I opened the ball with the "Gold and Silver Waltz" by Lehar. My husband said, "Waltz?" and I said, "Waltz!" He murmured, "One, two, three, one, two, three . . ." And I said, "No, darling. Spin at quarter time." And that was the last time I ever said, "Follow me, I shall lead." He never quite got over the dizzying speed of the waltz but it started our adventure in life together.' *Princess Michael*

'I don't give a toot for fashion. I just want to look nice.' *Princess Michael*

'She sounds far too grand for us.' *The Queen*

When it was revealed that her father had been a Nazi:
'I immediately telephoned my mother . . . and I said more or less to the effect, "Guess what they are trying to pin on me now?" And she said, "But I'm afraid that it is true." ' *Princess Michael*

'It was a total shock to everything I had been taught to believe.' *Princess Michael*

'It is like suddenly discovering you are adopted. Here I am, 40 years old, and I discover something that is really quite unpleasant and I shall have to live with it.' *Princess Michael*

'Because I have a handsome husband, two beautiful children, two beautiful houses and am a naturally happy person and because it appears I survive the blows directed against me, the blows get bigger and bigger.' *Princess Michael*

Describing her own physique:
'Tiny boobs and big shoulders.' *Princess Michael*

'I may be many things, but I'm not boring.' *Princess Michael*

'They need a soap opera to sell newspapers and they've got a hell of a soap opera with the Royal Family. They needed a bad girl and they've cast me in that role.' *Princess Michael*

'I don't think I'm really afraid of anything.' *Princess Michael*

'I am very keen on femininity, even though I am six foot and have large bones.' *Princess Michael*

'I have nothing against British clothes, but I am a foreign person and I have a foreign shape . . . And I don't believe in buying British if British isn't good enough.' *Princess Michael*

'The whole key to me is foreignness. But because I talk English like an English person, have English colouring, lead a very English life, people subconsciously expect me to be English in every way. But I'm not – I'm as foreign as could be.' *Princess Michael*

'I'm never unhappy. I'm momentarily unhappy, but I never allow myself to remain unhappy or depressed. I just go out and do something about it.' *Princess Michael*

Before making a public appearance:
'I always say a little prayer, "Please don't let me make a gaffe." ' *Princess Michael*

On her income:
'£70,000? I couldn't begin to live on that.' *Princess Michael*

Of herself and her husband:
'We'll go anywhere for a free meal.' *Princess Michael*

On a collection of Fabergé eggs she found while hunting out some spare furniture for her flat in the basement of Buckingham Palace:
'If I could just get my hands on one of those eggs, we'd be rich.' *Princess Michael*

'I have a better background than anyone else who's married into the Royal Family since the war, excepting Prince Philip.' *Princess Michael*

To the Prince and Princess of Wales, when she first visited Highgrove:
'What a beautiful house, but what a pity you didn't ask me to help redecorate it.' *Princess Michael*

'I tend to land on my feet. You see, I have this tremendous instinct for self-preservation.' *Princess Michael*

'I am on good terms with everybody.' *Princess Michael*

'Motormouth.' *Prince Philip's nickname for her*

'I am sometimes consumed with guilt at not spending enough time with the children. I don't think it is necessarily the amount of time you spend together if the time you do spend is quality time. When I am with them I focus, I zoom in on them. In those twenty minutes I do believe we get an awful lot across to each other.' *Princess Michael*

About her husband:
'He makes me nervous. You see, he wants me to win . . . I just want to survive.' *Princess Michael*

On her daughter, Lady Gabriella Windsor:
'She is already feminine and quite maternal. She seized her first doll with shrieks of delight.' *Princess Michael*

After the birth of her son, Lord Frederick Windsor:
'Look at his lovely big hands. He should make an excellent plumber.' *Princess Michael*

When he went to boarding school:
'Oh, he'll be OK. He's got my brains, thank heavens, and not the Kents.' *Princess Michael*

To her husband while the couple were posing for photographers:
'Try not to look stupid.' *Princess Michael*

Acknowledgements

We would like to extend our special thanks to Vida Adamoli, Jayne Lyle and Marie-Helene Canbos at Gamma Liaison who helped research the photographs.

We would also like to thank Harvey Weinig and Nicky Adamson for tasks too numerous to mention.

For help and assistance in our research we would like to extend our special gratitude to: Mary Davies, Sally O'Sullivan, John Haslam, Assistant Press Secretary to The Queen, the Press Office at Buckingham Palace, Jane Astell, Royal Liaison Assistant at Kensington House, BBC Press Office and The Jockey Club.

The following picture agencies all contributed to the gathering of photographs for this book: The Hulton Picture Company, Gamma Liaison, Frank Spooner, Syndication International, Mail/Solo, Nunn Syndication, Jayne Fincher at Photographers International, Michael Charity, Lionel Cherruault, Kent Gavin, Popperfoto, Daily Telegraph, Black and White Library, Associated Press, the Picture Desk of the Daily Mail, Sport and General press Agency and Eric Gibbs.

Special thanks to the authors of the following books: *Happy and Glorious! An Anthology of Royalty* edited by Peter Vansittart, *The Royals* by Jeannie Sakol and Caroline Latham, *The British Royal Family* by Anne Collins, *Majesty* by Robert Lacey, *Royal Children* by Celia Clear, *The Shy Princess* by David Duff, *King George VI* by Taylor Darbyshire, *King George VI: His Life and Reign* by Sir John Wheeler Bennett, *The Royal Gardeners: King George VI and His Queen* by W.E. Shewell-Cooper, *Queen Elizabeth, The Queen Mother* by Dorothy Laird, *The Queen Mother, The Queen: The Life of Elizabeth II* by Elizabeth Longford, *The Queen* by Ann Morrow, *Royal Britain in Queen Elizabeth's Silver Jubilee Year, 1977, Prince Philip, Duke of Edinburgh* by Dennis Judd, *Prince Philip* by Alan Hamilton, *The Duchess of Kent* by Helen Cathcart, *Anne, The Princess Royal* by Helen Cathcart, *HRH The Princess Anne A Biography* by Brian Hoey, *Diana* by Ingrid Seward, *Diana HRH The Princess of Wales* by Tim Graham, *Diana: The Fashion Princess* by Davina Hanmer, *Diana: Princess of Wales, Charles and Diana* by Ralph G. Martin, *Charles, Prince of Our Times* by Ronald Allison and Lemoine Serge, *Prince Charles* by Helen Cathcart, *Prince Charles* by Anthony Holden, *Charles* by Penny Junor, *The Prince of Wales* by W. Vaughan-Thomas, *Duchess* by Andrew Morton, *The Royal Family* by Sarah Litvinoff, *Utterly Trivial Knowledge* by Vida Adamoli.

We would also like to thank the following libraries, newspapers and magazines for helping with our research: The British Library at Colindale, Express Newspaper Library; the *Daily Express*, the *Daily Mail*, the *Daily Mirror*, *The Daily Telegraph*, the *Evening Standard*, *The Sun*, *The Times*, *Today*, *The Mail on Sunday*, the *News of the World*, the *Observer*, *The People*, the *Sunday Express*, the *Sunday Mirror*, *The Sunday Telegraph*, *The Sunday Times*, Peter Wells of *The Cambridge Evening News*, *Publishing News*, *Majesty*, *Palace*, *Royalty Monthly*, *Tatler*, *Vanity Fair*, *Harpers & Queen*, *Woman*, *Woman's Own*, *The Listener*, *New Statesman* and *Woman's Realm*.

Our thanks to John Dunn for his BBC radio 2 interview with HRH The Duchess of York, to Terry Wogan for his BBC1 television interview with HRH The Princess Anne, to Peter Williams for his interview on TVS television with Princess Anne, and to Brian Redhead for his interview on BBC radio 4's 'Today' programme with The Prince of Wales.

It has not been possible in all cases to trace the copyright sources, and we would be glad to hear from any such unacknowledged copyright holder.

Publisher May 1990